DATE DUE

DISCARDED

Demco, Inc. 38-293

The Dynamics of Organizational Collapse

'This book investigates the events from Nick Leeson's employment with Barings in Singapore in 1992 to Barings' collapse in 1995, generating valuable insights based on a high-level multi-theoretical analysis involving psychological and sociological theories. It is a must-read and an insightful organizational behaviour analysis. I recommend it to all who are interested in a general psychological and sociological theory of how and why organizations fail.'

Ted Azarmi (California State University, Long Beach, USA)

The collapse of Barings Bank was a commercial catastrophe that resonated worldwide, showing what kind of secrets can lie behind an apparently successful organization. Following Nick Leeson's arrest and subsequent conviction for fraud, investment banks anxiously reviewed their risk management controls to make sure that it could never happen again.

Helga Drummond's exploration is conducted against a backdrop of social and psychological theories of decision error that seeks to go beyond media style accusations of greed and incompetence. She challenges the myth that Barings 'must have known' that mischief was afoot. The book offers lessons for all organizations as it shows how easily managers can end up living in a world of fantasy believing that everything is under control when the precise opposite may be true. It is not risk and uncertainty that should worry organizations, concludes Drummond, but what they are most sure of.

The collapse of Barings Bank had international ramifications, and this scholarly analysis will have an international audience as a result. The book will be of great interest to all those interested in social psychology, the application of psychology in management theory, sociology and organizational behaviour. It is also suitable as recommended reading for a management or organization behaviour course.

Helga Drummond is Professor of Decision Sciences at the University of Liverpool Management School.

Routledge international studies in money and banking

The Dynamics of Organizational Collapse

The case of Barings Bank

Helga Drummond

Routledge
Taylor & Francis Group

NEW YORK AND LONDON

First published 2008
by Routledge
2 Park Square, Milton Park, Abingdon, Oxon, OX14 4RN

Simultaneously published in the USA and Canada
by Routledge
270 Madison Ave, New York NY 10016

*Routledge is an imprint of the Taylor & Francis Group,
an informa business*

Transferred to Digital Printing 2009

© 2008 Helga Drummond

Typeset in Times New Roman by Keyword Group Ltd

British Library Cataloguing in Publication Data
A catalogue record for this book is available from the British Library

Library of Congress Cataloging in Publication Data
Drummond, Helga.
 The dynamics of organizational collapse: the case of Barings Bank /
 Helga Drummond.
 p. cm.
 Includes bibliographical references and index.
 1. Barings Bank. 2. Bank failures—Great Britain. 3. Merchant banks—
 Great Britain. 4. Leeson, Nicholas William. 5. Organizational behavior—
 Case studies. 6. Corporate culture—Case studies. 7. Organizational
 effectiveness—Case studies. I. Title.
 HG2998.B35D78 2008
 332.1′20941—dc22
 2007028584

ISBN10: 0-415-39961-0 (hbk)
ISBN10: 0-203-93277-3 (ebk)

ISBN13: 978-0-415-39961-6 (hbk)
ISBN13: 978-0-203-93277-3 (ebk)

For Gannon Drummond, William Drummond, Alexander Drummond and Dominic Drummond

Contents

Preface

I was at home enjoying a quiet Sunday morning pot of coffee when I first heard the news on the radio that Barings was rumoured to be in serious trouble. I did not pay much attention to the item or the subsequent manhunt for the missing trader as I was busy writing a book about another City fiasco, namely the collapse of TAURUS, a large-scale IT project sponsored by the London Stock Exchange. It was only during the summer of 1996, after the book was finished, that I became interested as I sat by a stream on holiday and read Leeson's story named *Rogue Trader*.

I was then fortunate to be awarded a grant by the Economic and Science Research Council (ESRC) to delve more deeply into events. This exploration was followed by Terry Clague's invitation to write this book. When I applied for financial support to ESRC, I made it clear that this was to be a textual study. Key actors could not be interviewed at the time because of pending court cases, or in Leeson's case because they were in custody. To have interviewed some people and not others would have been to deny some actors a voice and distorted the account. It was all or nothing.

I gratefully acknowledge assistance I have received from accountants, bankers and lawyers, all of whom wish to remain anonymous. I am also grateful to Chris Thomas, formerly of the Bank of England's library (since closed), for access to parliamentary reports that I might otherwise have been unaware of. Janet Briddon carefully checked the text – the remaining errors are mine.

Much has happened since I sat reading by the stream. I now have four nephews ever ready to relieve me of my small change and in whose company reading seems a waste of time and is in any case impossible.

Principal actors

James Baker	Internal Auditor
Ron Baker	Head of Financial Products Group
Peter Baring	Chairman of Barings
James Bax	Head of South Asia
Gordon Bowser	Risk Manager, Barings Securities
Geoff Broadhurst	Group Finance Director, Barings Investment Bank
Tony Gamby	Settlements Director
Brenda Granger	Manager of Futures and Options Settlement
Fernando Gueler	Senior Trader in Osaka
Tony Hawes	Group Treasurer of Barings Investment Bank
Ian Hopkins	Director, Group Head Treasury and Risk
Simon Jones	Director, Barings Futures Singapore and Chief Operating Officer for South Asia
Nick Leeson	Manager, Barings Futures Singapore
Peter Norris	Chief Executive of Barings Investment Bank
Tony Railton	Futures and Options Settlement Clerk
Valerie Thomas	Head of Compliance
Andrew Tuckey	Deputy Chairman of Barings and Chairman of Baring Brothers
Mary Waltz	Global Head of Equity Financial Products

Summary of key events

July 1989	Leeson joins Barings as a settlements clerk initially based in London.
February 1992	Barings applies to Financial Services Authority to have Leeson licensed to trade financial contracts. Leeson makes a false statement on his application.
March 1992	Leeson seconded to Singapore.
3 July 1992	Leeson opens error account number '88888'.
21 July 1992	Leeson applies to Singapore International Monetary Exchange (SIMEX) for licence to trade financial contracts and again makes a false statement on the application.
24 March 1993	Christopher Heath resigns from Barings. Peter Norris becomes Chief Executive.
Late 1993	Ron Baker becomes Head of Financial Products Group. Leeson's trading activities come within his purview.
November 1993	Barings becomes 'solo-consolidated' for accounting purposes. This effectively means there are no constraints upon the amount of money that could be remitted to Singapore to support Leeson's trading.
July 1994	Internal audit of Singapore office begins.
October 1994	Internal audit report circulated to senior management.
11 January 1995	SIMEX query margin requirements for account 88888.
14 January 1995	External auditors discover £50 million discrepancy in Singapore accounts and subsequently spend two weeks trying to extract an explanation from Leeson about so-called 'SLK receivable'.
17 January 1995	Kobe earthquake.
24 January 1995	Asset and Liability Committee (ALCO) instructs Leeson to reduce positions because of funding pressure. ALCO also notes inaccurate reporting of margin requirements. Daily income report suggests Leeson made over £3 million in a single day.
27 January 1995	SIMEX queries adequacy of funds to meet margin calls.

30 January 1995	News of alleged 'SLK receivable' reaches London. There is confusion about what has happened. Bombastic conversations between Ron Baker and Tony Hawes ensue.
31 January 1995	Year end bonus for Andrew Tuckey is £1.65 million. Ron Baker due to receive £800,000 and Leeson £450,000.
2 February 1995	Tony Railton instructed not to get involved in so-called 'SLK transaction' when he visits Singapore.
3 February 1995	James Bax faxes Peter Norris, advising that Leeson will no longer be responsible for settling transactions.
6 February 1995	Tony Railton starts work in Singapore, initially supported by Tony Hawes.
6 February 1995	Diarmid Kelly tells Management Committee that no one makes US$9 million in a week without risk. Management Committee is aware of market rumour.
8 February 1995	Peter Norris directs that ALCO minutes on the SLK transaction be kept very brief.
13 February 1995	Alleged 'SLK receivable' reported to Management Committee as an 'operational error'.
15 February 1995	James Bax instructs Simon Jones to extricate Leeson from SLK 'loop' and 'take on' Tony Hawes himself.
16 February 1995	Peter Norris visits Singapore. Meets with Leeson for about forty minutes.
17 February 1995	Tony Railton informs Brenda Granger and Tony Gamby that he is unable to reconcile Leeson's accounts. There appears to be a £100 million discrepancy. Railton is instructed to continue his efforts to reconcile the accounts. Schroders inform Barings of a rumour suggesting overexposure to a counterparty.
19 February 1995	Ron Baker interrupts his holiday to forcibly instruct Leeson not to increase positions.
22 February 1995	Plc Board meets, attended by Mr Tuckey, Mr Norris and others. Board notes that in 1994 Leeson made £12.7 million, whereas Barings Investment Bank as a whole made only £8.486 million.
23 February 1995	Tony Hawes describes Leeson's request for an additional US$100 million as incomprehensible given that positions were to be reduced. Leeson's mysterious disappearance is reported to Tony Gamby in London. Peter Norris assembles a small team to investigate.
24 February 1995	Printout of account 88888 discovered lying on Leeson's desk reveals thousands of unauthorized trades, all losing money.
26 February 1995	Barings declared insolvent.

Introduction

> The ... account showed a shocking disparity between what they thought Leeson had been doing and the truth ... The daily reports they had received from him had been complete fiction. [They] had met daily and solemnly discussed the profits and supposed tiny risks of Leeson's trading. But all this had been a fantasy.
>
> (*All that Glitters*, Gapper and Denton 1996: 29)

On Thursday 23 February 1995 the directors of Barings Bank hosted a lunch for City magnates. The conversation was animated, much of it focused on Barings' new venture in Mexico. 'They had no idea,' said a guest afterwards.

Financial markets in the Far East had been ablaze for weeks about the bank's potentially catastrophic exposure to risk. Yet the directors (who knew about the rumours) had 'no idea' that Barings, one of the oldest and most respectable houses in the City of London, was about to collapse.

Around four o'clock that afternoon Peter Norris, Chief Executive of Barings Investment Bank, learned that Nick Leeson, the bank's star trader based in Singapore, had mysteriously disappeared amidst an inquiry into a £100 million 'hole' in his accounts. Norris immediately assembled a task force to investigate. Meanwhile, Leeson's colleagues in Singapore began casually leafing through papers on his desk (Ministry for Finance, Singapore 1995). They came across a bank statement that looked suspicious. The statement showed that £50 million had been paid into an account and the transaction immediately reversed. Why should anyone do that? The sum of money, moreover, matched a sale that Leeson claimed to have made to a firm of brokers named Spear, Leeds and Kellogg (SLK) a few weeks ago. The so-called 'SLK transaction' had caused uproar when it was reported to London by the external auditors because Leeson had no authority to trade financial contracts 'over the counter'. To make matters worst, Leeson had apparently forgotten to collect payment, leaving Barings owed £50 million by a firm whose credit rating was unknown because no checks had been made. The discovery of the bank statement together with the knowledge of the missing £100 million and Leeson's mysterious disappearance sounded alarm bells. Had Leeson been stealing money?

Worse was to come. The computer printout on Leeson's desk was designated 'error account number 88888'. Error accounts are used to store failed trades, for example, if a contract to buy is wrongly executed as a contract to sell. In the normal course of business, such accounts would be expected to contain around thirty or forty transactions. As Leeson's colleagues began turning the pages, they soon realized that it was actually a trading account. The account showed that Leeson had been selling highly risky financial contracts known as options without Barings' knowledge or authority – thousands of them. Moreover, every contract was losing money – literally by the second (Gapper and Denton 1996: 27). During the night it became apparent that Barings was virtually insolvent.

Next morning the directors held an emergency meeting. After taking legal advice, Barings continued trading on the Friday. A rescue attempt was then mounted over the weekend and potential buyers discreetly approached. The attempt failed and on Monday morning Barings passed into the hands of the administrators and ultimately into history. Leeson's losses eventually totalled over £900 million – double the bank's capital base of about £480 million. Barings was eventually sold to the Dutch bank ING for a nominal sum of one pound. The fall from grace was brilliantly encapsulated by a cartoon published by the *Financial Times* newspaper. The cartoon depicts two tramps sitting on a pavement begging for money with upturned caps. One tramp says to the other, 'Soon I'll have enough to buy Barings.'

Aims of this book

Barings' sudden and utter collapse was a commercial catastrophe. It showed what may lie behind an apparently successful organization and highlighted the ever present shadow of systemic risk to the entire banking system. The significance of the catastrophe is reflected in the two official inquiries one in the UK (Board of Banking Supervision 1995) and one in Singapore (Ministry for Finance, Singapore 1995) plus a series of ad hoc investigations by the Treasury Committee of the UK parliament. In addition, several books have been written (e.g. Fay 1996; Gapper and Denton 1996; Rawnsley 1996) about Barings, including Leeson's (1997) own account, written with the assistance of Edward Whitley. In addition the collapse has been widely reported in the media. So the question arises, why another book when so much is already known?

First and foremost, my purpose is different from that of a regulator or a journalist. Regulators are interested in apportioning blame for what happened and in drawing the obvious lessons. Journalists want to tell a story of greed and monumental incompetence. While we can learn a great deal from their work, my purpose is to try and get beyond the obvious and journalists' parsimonious explanations of greed and incompetence by exploring the organizational and social-psychological dynamics of the story in order to understand why it could happen again. Indeed it *has* happened again.

In 2004 China Aviation Oil lost $550 million when rising oil prices exposed reckless bets made by traders in oil derivatives working on SIMEX. A few years earlier Allied Irish Banks lost $691 million due to hidden losses at a US subsidiary incurred by a currency trader named John Rusnak. The episode resonated with events in Barings, that is, a trader working in a remote location with little supervision dealing with exotic financial contracts. Allied Irish Bank survived because its capital base was bigger than Barings – otherwise history might have repeated itself (Larsen 2005a, 2005b).

In addition, there are lessons to be learned for organizations generally. As we shall see later in this book, there are echoes of Barings in a wide range of organizational failures, including the collapse of Enron, Shell's overstatement of reserves, Deloitte's ill-advised law suit against the Bank of England, Cadbury's admission of selling contaminated chocolate bars and the failure of the UK authorities to follow up leads that might have prevented the London Tube bombings of 2005 (e.g. Moore et al. 2006; O'Neill and McGrory 2006; Tait 2005; Whyte 1991b).

Psychologists are sometimes accused of telling people what they already know in language they don't understand. Sociologists are perhaps even worse, deploying abstruse and verbose language to say very little. Indeed, some of my conclusions drawn after paragraphs of analysis may say little more than 'greed and incompetence' in polite language. Yet I doubt whether Barings' senior managers saw themselves as greedy. In fact, Barings was risk averse as a matter of policy. Moreover, although decision-makers at the strategic apex of the organization may have had insufficient knowledge of the securities business they were surrounded by experts. Why did they not seek and/or receive advice?

For all their limitations, the theories invoked in this book highlight the limits of commonsense and suggest why the obvious does not always happen in organizations. For example, latterly Barings was confronted by at least six clear warning signs of malfeasance. These were:

- Huge profits from allegedly risk-free trading.
- Trading rising when it was supposed to be falling.
- Unreconciled balances in accounts involved over £90 million, latterly escalating demands for collateral (margin), and Leeson's failure to explain how those monies were being used.
- The discovery of the so-called unauthorized trade worth £50 million.
- The fact that Leeson controlled both trading and subsequent processing known as settlement.
- The emergence of market rumour.

The Board of Banking Supervision (1995) concluded that while those signs might not have meant much in isolation, together they should have triggered alarm. Our theories help us to understand why in fact the precise opposite happened.

After Barings collapsed it was widely suggested in the popular press and by some scholarly commentators like David Kynaston (2001) and the Singapore official inquiry (Ministry for Finance, Singapore 1995) that Barings must have had some inkling of the truth. For example, the Singapore authorities cite the speed with which Leeson's unauthorized trades were discovered as evidence of conspiracy. Barings certainly knew that Leeson's alleged trading was at the margins of legality because it involved 'front running' customers – a form of insider trading. Barings may also have suspected that Leeson was breaking his trading limits. Moreover, transcripts of recorded telephone conversations between key actors during the final weeks of the bank's existence suggest that they were baffled by certain aspects of Leeson's behaviour and may have been edging their way towards the truth (see especially Gapper and Denton 1996).

Aside from those observations the evidence clearly shows that Barings was taken completely by surprise. Indeed, the most intriguing aspect of the bank's collapse and the stimulus to research it and write about it was the gap between what senior and middle managers understood and believed to be true and the reality. It is that gap that makes analysis interesting and provides the focal point for this book. How did that gap arise and what sustained it?

Approach to analysis

Each phase of the story starts with an explanation of the theory that will be invoked to subsequently analyse it. The story is then told. Analysis follows in a separate chapter. As far as possible I have avoided jargon. Terms like 'structuration' and 'representativeness' appear only where it is necessary to locate theory intellectually. A more 'user friendly' terminology has then been substituted.

I have tried to make the telling of the story as interesting as possible while feeling inadequate beside some of the excellent accounts that have been written by journalists. These include John Gapper and Michael Denton's *All that Glitters* (1996), a most lucid and authoritative account based in part upon transcripts of recorded telephone conversations. Stephen Fay's *The Collapse of Barings* (1996) is richly detailed and highly readable. There is also Leeson's own account *Rogue Trader* (1996) written with the assistance of Edward Whitley. The latter is a gripping read but it should be noted that Leeson's claim that his problems started through trying to protect a young clerk from being dismissed for making a mistake is inconsistent with evidence obtained by official inquiries. That evidence shows that Leeson's misuse of the error account started months earlier.

I have tried to keep the story simple. The reader interested in knowing precisely how many contracts Leeson held, for example, in Japanese Government Bonds on a particular day or the difference between variation margin and intra-day margin should consult the official reports issued by the Board of Banking Supervision (1995) and the Ministry for Finance, Singapore (1995). I have consistently used the term options to describe Leeson's trading without delving into the intricacies of the role of straddles, ticks and so forth. More precise details are contained in the official inquiries and also in Stonham's (1996a, 1996b) useful overview.

Validity of sources

The inquiry conducted by the Board of Banking Supervision did not have access to all the evidence available to the authorities in Singapore and vice versa. Between them the two reports provide a comprehensive account of events that has never been challenged on the basis of fact. The report issued by the Board of Banking Supervision forms the mainstay of this book. To save repeated referencing, the reader can assume this is the source unless otherwise stated. I have also had access to unpaginated transcripts of evidence given in court. The court proceedings largely repeat the findings of the Board of Banking Supervision but where they have added detail or additional explanation I have referred to them. I applied the same principle to utilizing evidence given to Treasury Committees. I have drawn on Leeson's (1996) book, Gapper and Denton (1996) and Fay (1996) to construct the chronology and to convey something of the atmosphere in Barings as events unfolded.

All accounts are biased. The Singapore inquiry, for example, criticizes Barings for failing to ensure that only properly qualified staff were allowed to trade on the Singapore International Monetary Exchange (SIMEX). Yet the report is less forthcoming in its criticism of SIMEX for its favourable treatment of Leeson who was named 'trader of the year' in 1994 in recognition of the amount of new business generated for the fledgling exchange.

Andrew Brown (2005; see also Hall 1995) is scathing about the Board of Banking Supervision inquiry. For all its measured language, says Brown, the primary aim of the report is to protect the financial services industry generally and the Bank of England in particular from criticism. This book certainly challenges some of the recommendations for practice made by the Board of Banking Supervision. I also suggest that some of the criticisms levied against individuals for failing to do their jobs fail to take adequate account of the factors that undermined the effectiveness of those individuals. I also accord considerably more emphasis to Leeson's licence application than the Board of Banking Supervision, which dealt with it in a short paragraph under a section entitled 'Other Matters'. The paragraph reads:

> Leeson's application in March 1992 for SFA [Securities and Futures Authority] registration as a securities representative failed to mention a small unsatisfied County Court judgement debt which had recently been obtained against him. The SFA made enquiries of Barings about it, but the issue lapsed because the application was not pursued.
>
> (Board of Banking Supervision 1995: 228)

Leeson's failure to mention the debt meant that he might have lied on his application form. Yet the Board of Banking Supervision made no criticism of the Financial Services Authority (FSA) for allowing the issue to lapse instead of demanding a report from Barings about what action had been taken to investigate this potentially disturbing revelation.

The reader in search of an in-depth analysis of Leeson's motivation may be disappointed. While Leeson played an important role in the bank's downfall, it is an exaggeration to suggest that Barings was destroyed by one man. By his own admission Leeson was motivated by an ambition to become a trader and fear of the loss of status he would suffer if he was no longer 'in the money'. Suffice be it to say that in 1993 Leeson managed to clear his losses but continued his reckless options trading because he needed the intoxicant of success (Leeson 1997; see also Ross 1997).

The reader seeking a detailed analysis of the auditors' role and analysis of issues pertaining to international regulation may likewise find me wanting. While those factors undoubtedly contributed to Barings' collapse, my focus is mainly upon what happened within Barings and the lessons to be drawn for other organizations.

Structure

Chapters 1, 2 and 3 examine the circumstances surrounding Leeson's aforementioned licence application. The theory set out in Chapter 1 focuses mainly upon the potentially paradoxical nature of organization dynamics and how activity that is a means to an end can become an end in itself with unexpected and unwanted consequences.

Chapter 2 opens with a short account of the history of the bank and how Barings almost collapsed in 1890. The story then moves forward ninety years and briefly explains Barings' decision taken in the early 1980s to diversify into the securities industry. It was an experiment that exceeded expectations and helped ensure the bank's survival in the post deregulation (Big Bang) era, but the underdeveloped administrative infrastructure provided a breeding ground for malfeasance. The main part of the chapter concerns Leeson's two applications to be licensed to trade financial contracts and how Leeson obtained a licence despite being potentially ineligible.

Chapter 3 analyses how and why it happened. Organizations clearly require rules and regulations to guide action thereby minimizing the need for referral. Yet the results may be different from what the organization intended because someone has to decide when, where and how to apply the rules. What happens, moreover, when the rules are silent or ambiguous? Conceivably culture can provide an important backdrop for dealing with unprecedented situations. That line of defence failed in the present study because the ethos in Barings reflected a merchant banking culture that was insensitive to the risks involved in running a securities business.

Speculation existed when Barings collapsed that Leeson had an accomplice. He did and the miscreant has never been brought to justice and never will be because they are beyond the jurisdiction of any court. The next three chapters examine the role played by that accomplice in deceiving Barings – the computer.

Chapter 4 considers how relatively lowly actors like Leeson can acquire power above and beyond their role prescription. We begin by introducing notions of agency and explain how the organization's dependency on employees as agents to execute the directives affords a measure of autonomy and with it the option of acting differently from what the organization intends. We then consider how autonomy may be enhanced through access to people, resources and instrumentalities and the ambiguity of structure. Chapter 5 considers how Leeson created and exploited dependency to open a secret account on the computer – number 88888. Singaporeans are superstitious. Leeson chose the number 8 because it is considered lucky: it means 'to prosper'. The number 5, however, is considered unlucky because it means 'never'. The 'never prosper account' (Gapper and Denton 1996) was subsequently used by Leeson to hide his illicit options trading.

Chapter 6 analyses those developments. What emerges shows how controls intended to limit opportunism can actually facilitate it. Account 88888 need not have remained a secret, however. Details eventually appeared in a suspense file held in London but the file was never audited.

Chapters 7, 8 and 9 consider the development of Leeson's power and the script change from occupying the role of mere order filler to his emergence as Barings' star trader (see also Greener 2006). Chapter 7 builds upon the theme of informal power by invoking Giddens' (1979, 1984) work on the dynamics of organizational structure. Chapter 8 recounts how Leeson changed the script. The analysis contained in Chapter 9 highlights the subtly shifting tides of organization as it shows how shows how profound change can occur in ways that almost imperceptible and are therefore well nigh impossible for managers to control. By the time Barings realized what was happening in Singapore, Leeson was well and truly entrenched and a force to be reckoned with, as the internal auditors discovered. This chapter also anticipates psychological theories used mainly to analyse later phases of the story suggesting that Leeson was partly protected by the reluctance of internal auditors (and other powerful actors) to admit that they did not understand his trading strategy.

Chapters 10, 11 and 12 explore events during the final weeks of Barings' existence. Chapter 10 provides the theoretical backdrop drawing upon psychological, social and organizational theories of decision error. Chapter 11 tells the story of those final weeks. We see how Leeson's losses spiralled out of control, forcing Barings to remit more and more of its precious capital to support trading it did not even know existed. Reference is also made to the discovery of the so-called 'SLK transaction' – a serious breach of discipline. Had it been dealt with properly, the bank would have been saved.

Chapter 12 analyses the widening gap between fantasy and reality. It begins by considering what can plausibly be explained as a failure of sense-making in an unprecedented situation. The focus of attention then shifts to the protocols and procedures (known as action generators: Starbuck 1983) used by management to make decisions, and how they distorted impressions. We also see how warning signs were missed by key actors rationalizing potentially ominous information to fit their expectations. The pivotal point, however, is political, as powerful factions support Leeson in order to deflect attention from their managerial failings, destroying important organizational checks and balances in the process.

Chapters 13, 14 and 15 consider the role played by Barings' most senior decision-makers, the Management Committee (MANCO), as the last line of defence. Chapter 13 explains the various theories of what psychologists call 'the illusion of control', that is, our innate capacity as human beings to overestimate our abilities (e.g. Pfeffer and Fong 2005), including a phenomenon known as 'groupthink' whereby groups can become a liability if members avoid challenging one another for fear of upsetting the cohesive atmosphere.

Chapter 14 begins by backtracking to September 1993 and Peter Baring's pleasure in the apparently 'amazing' recovery of the securities business. The most crucial part of the story concerns a meeting on 6 February 1995, when Diarmid Kelly warns colleagues that no one makes $9 million in a week without taking some kind of risk. It was one of the last chances to save the bank but the warning was politely ignored, even though MANCO was aware of rumours suggesting that Barings was already 'bust'.

Barings drew an important lesson from events of 1890. Barings decided that never again would the bank's capital be put at risk. In theory, such low risk propensity should have led to the Management Committee being overly sensitive to risk – seeing danger where none existed instead of becoming exposed to catastrophic levels of risk (Sitkin and Pablo 1992; Sitkin and Weingart 1995). Chapter 15 analyses this conundrum. It is concluded that while Barings may have been greedy, its blindness to reality reflected a deeper insecurity (see also Stein 2000).

Chapter 16, the last in the book, opens with a brief recapitulation and then discusses the implications for theory and practice. The most important lesson is that what we call 'reality' in organizations is a myth, partly true and therefore partly untrue. Much has been said in the wake of Barings' collapse about the need for organizations to grapple with risk and danger. Yet it is not uncertainty that should worry managers so much as that which they know and believe to be true.

1 The paradox of consequences

For thirteen days in October 1962 the world stood poised on the brink of a nuclear holocaust following the discovery by US spy planes of rocket launch pads under construction in Cuba. During the crisis the US government executive committee met daily and spent long hours deliberating the problem, analysing options and discussing how to obtain Russia's consent to the removal of the rocket sites without losing international prestige. During that critical period one of President Kennedy's worst fears was that the holocaust would be triggered not by heads of state taking a clear and volitional decision to exercise grave options, but by an inexorable chain of events triggered by a low ranking operative carrying out their duties in a normal fashion responding to pre-programmed events (Allison and Zelikow 1999).

Kennedy was right to be afraid. Large events do not always have large causes. We begin by considering a small but significant failure of control that occurred before Leeson actually reached Singapore. Leeson should never have been allowed to trade financial contracts in the first place because he failed a background check. Yet those responsible for administering the initial background check followed the system. Moreover, the system worked as intended in that it identified Leeson as potentially ineligible to be licensed. Yet Leeson was able to trade with impunity under the noses of compliance officers whose duty it was to ensure that only properly qualified persons were allowed to gain access to the trading floor. How and why did it happen?

Why do organizations exist?

In order to explain why control in organizations is seldom perfect, it is necessary to step back and remind ourselves why organizations exist in the first place. This question is preceded by another. Why put locks on doors? Probably only burglars and economists ever think about it! An economist might say that locks are fitted only where the value of the room's contents justifies the cost of purchasing, fitting and subsequently maintaining the lock.

Likewise, why go to the bother of creating an organization? In a seminal contribution, Williamson (1975, 1981, 1991; see also Ouchi 1980) argues that organizations take over where market transactions break down. According to Williamson, markets are efficient where transactions are predictable and easy to control. For example, contracts for selling commodities are amenable to market transactions because coffee beans, gold, silver, hogs and so forth can be graded according to weight and quality with simple formulae being applied to calculate price adjustments for minor variations. Markets offer the cheapest way of doing business because the transaction costs are minimal. All that is required is that a willing buyer meets a willing seller and that simple ground rules are agreed between them. For example, commodities markets use formulae for calculating price adjustments where say the weight of a particular batch of hogs is slightly below industry standards.

According to Williamson, markets fail in conditions of high uncertainty and/or where transactions are complex and contract performance is difficult to regulate therefore giving rise to increased potential for opportunism. Opportunism means the seeking of self-interest with guile – including lying, stealing and cheating. In this view bureaucracy in the form of hierarchical control, rule books and so forth supported by mechanisms of surveillance are like fitting locks on doors, a legitimate business expense aimed at discouraging would-be opportunists.

Another view of organizations is that they exist because they can achieve what would either be impossible or hopelessly inefficient by an individual working alone (see, for example, the sustained critique of Williamson's work by Ghoshal and Moran 1996). In this view organizations exist to achieve certain goals and bureaucracy enables organizations to accomplish their goals with maximum efficiency (Weber1947; see also Blau 1956; Crozier 1964).

Rationality is the key to maximizing efficiency. Rationality means calculation of the most efficient means of accomplishing a particular end. It is not a new idea. Medieval monastic foundations utilized rational methods of production in order to maximize the time for prayer. For example, the monks used forecasting models for bread, 'The number is always the same, unless through some accident there should be a need for fewer rations; for there is never a need for more' (Keiser 1987: 112).

The next step was the invention of systems of mass production. Hitherto a pin maker might produce one pin a day. A system whereby 'One man draws out the wire, another straightens it, a third cuts it, a fourth points it' (Smith 1983:110) could enable labourers in a small manufactory to produce twelve pounds of pins in one day – provided they exerted themselves that is. Management's most influential exponent of rationality was F. W. Taylor. Taylor (1947) recommended separating conception of work from its actual execution, that is, management assumes control of work processes and methods, while employees merely discharge their allotted tasks. Tasks moreover were deskilled, that is, divided into miniscule components to facilitate rapid accomplishment and to require minimal training or knowledge thereby minimizing expense and rendering operatives dispensable.

Specialization means coordination is required so that all the subdivided tasks come together as a coherent whole. In a small organization, coordination can be achieved through interpersonal contact and informal agreements about what should be done. In a large organization this becomes impossible and so more formal mechanisms of communication and control are required. These typically take the form of managerial responsibility exercised through a hierarchy of authority. In theory hierarchies serve to create lines of communication between the upper and lower echelons of organization so that information can flow upwards and downwards and directives can be communicated. In practice, as we shall see later, hierarchies also serve to insulate the higher echelons from what is happening at the lower echelons.

Another feature of bureaucracies is an elaborate framework of rules. Rules serve to create consistency and obviate the need for constant referral – thus helping to minimize cost. For instance, a defining feature of bureaucracy is that if you ask two administrators the same question, such as, 'What rate of mileage can I claim as expenses for using my car on official business?', each administrator should give the same answer. Better still, the enquirer can consult the rule book and check the answer for themselves.

Impersonality means that the enquirer gets paid the correct mileage allowance regardless of whether the person processing claim likes them or not. The person processing the claim cannot say, 'I hate Mr Smith so instead of paying him the official rate of sixty pence a mile I will give him nothing.' Nor can they say, 'Sixty pence a mile is far too much! I will only pay ten pence a mile.'

Bureaucracy in practice

We are not concerned with the allegedly dehumanizing aspects of bureaucracy and its applications via Taylorism (for a critique see, for example, Braverman 1974). The point at issue here is why organizations fail despite (or perhaps because of) the discipline and regularity that bureaucracy imposes. Police and intelligence services proved powerless to prevent the attacks on the London Underground system that killed fifty-two innocent people in July 2005 and then two weeks later shot dead an innocent bystander named Jean Charles de Menezes in a bungled surveillance operation. The UK government spends billions of pounds annually on defence, yet combat troops are being sent to dangerous places like Afghanistan and Iraq allegedly without basic equipment. Nor do public sector bureaucracies possess a monopoly on fiasco. Audi invested millions of pounds in its flagship TT sports car. Yet early production models concealed unreliable electrics and a potentially lethal design fault whereby the car could become unstable at high speeds. More recently Sony is being sued for selling potentially dangerous batteries to computer manufacturers like Dell.

In theory, rational bureaucratic organizations offer four key interrelated benefits, namely efficiency, predictability, calculability and control by enabling organizations to deliver goods and services of uniform quality and quantity, via a production system that maximizes output for a given cost (Ritzer 1993). Those benefits come at a price, however. Merton (1936) argues that bureaucracy as a system of action almost inevitably generates side effects that contradict its basic objectives. System of action means the discipline needed for standardized behaviour to be observed. In this view although organizations may be deflected by actors breaking the rules, they may also be undermined by actors adhering to orders.

To begin with, in practice, control in organizations is seldom perfect because, for one reason or another, actors depart from procedure. When Menezes emerged from his flat in Brixton in South London, the undercover police officer who identified him as a potential suicide bomber had gone to urinate behind some bushes and was therefore unable to switch on his camera that would have enabled him to share information with colleagues in command control.

The result of following procedures, however, can be a paradox of consequences known as 'the irrationality of rationality' whereby rational systems produce results that are patently absurd and even tragic (Ritzer 1993; see also Drummond 1998b; Watson 1994). The intellectual vehicle for exploring this proposition is the trope of irony. The word 'trope' is derived from the Greek language meaning 'turn, twist' (Gibbs 1993; Manning 1979; Morgan 1980, 1983). Tropes provide a form of notation for telling reality in a particular way in order to facilitate the conceptualization of experience (Brown 1989; Watson 1994). To be more precise, what is seen in data depends upon the conceptual lens used to analyse it. This is because different analytical perspectives define differently what are to be taken as the basic 'facts' of the situation (e.g. Brown 1989, 1977; Morgan 1990). The reader may be most familiar with the trope of metonymy. Metonymy reflects a positivist view of the science which approaches the study of social phenomena in the same way as the natural sciences (e.g. Brown 1989; Burrell and Morgan 1979; Giddens 1995). Metonymy expresses contiguous relations between objects such as cause and effect with its root metaphor of mechanism (e.g. Brown 1989; Gibbs 1993; Morgan 1980). For example, what causes occupational stress?

Irony is defined as a 'reflective form of metaphorical imagination that involves the interplay of opposites and creates insight through paradox and contradiction' (Brown 1977: 172). What all ironies have in common is that they are a structure of ambiguities and contradictions that are revealed over time as events ripen to yield an unexpected yet inevitable outcome. Strictly speaking, if something is inevitable it can hardly be unexpected. Analysis seeks to penetrate this paradox by focusing upon the structure of contradictions inherent in the situation itself in order to explain the contrast between expectations and outcomes.

Ironically it is frequently the very strengths of bureaucracy that turn out to be its most dangerous weakness. Being rule governed implies inflexibility – hence President Kennedy's fear of a nuclear holocaust being triggered by someone at the lower echelons executing their routines. As soon as Menezes was identified as a terrorist suspect, an armed response unit was dispatched with orders to stop him from boarding a tube train. Shortly afterwards officers commanding the operation officers began to harbour doubts about whether Menezes posed a terrorist threat after all. Unlike the suicide bombers of 7 July, Menezes was not carrying a rucksack. Moreover, he was wearing only a light denim jacket and therefore unlikely to be concealing explosives. By then, however, the armed response unit was pursuing Menezes down the escalator of Stockwell tube station. Their radios did not work underground. Menezes stopped to pick up a free newspaper from a stand at the bottom of the escalator (another unlikely act for someone intent upon a suicide mission) and began running as he sighted a train about to leave. Two police officers entered the carriage where Menezes was sitting. Stopping a terrorist who might be about to trigger a lethal explosion leaves no room for asking questions. The drill was carried out in a textbook fashion – exactly according to the rules of engagement. One officer pinned Menezes by the arms, another shot him seven times through the head. The moment the unfortunate Menezes boarded the train he was almost literally a dead man.

Inflexibility is not the only problem created by bureaucracy. Recall, irony focuses our attention upon opposites. It exposes chaos in what appears to be order, order in what appears to be chaotic, differences in things that appear to be similar, similarities in things that appear to be different. Bureaucratic organizations are prone to a phenomenon known as means/ends reversal or the so-called 'paradox of consequences' whereby the application of rules, protocols and procedures becomes an end in itself with the result that the organization becomes deflected from its overarching purpose (Drummond 1996, 2001; Watson 1994; Watzlawick et al. 1974).

Just as our attempts to create order can produce chaos, speed cameras can create danger as motorists suddenly slow down in order to avoid detection. Moreover, cameras can create a preoccupation with catching and fining erring motorists. Consequently the overarching goal of promoting road safety through good driving techniques and so forth gets forgotten. Doctors spend so much time carrying out tests in order to satisfy the requirements of clinical governance that they no longer talk to their patients. Classroom teachers can spend so much time on paperwork that their inspiration as teachers dries up. Moreover, the actual form filling can become an end in itself – something that has to be done in order to satisfy a third party and gets done in an unreflective manner. The pressure to produce results may also create a temptation to take shortcuts:

> Even the most brilliant and impeccably ethical leader of any large organization will eventually develop some skeletons in the closet because of the nature of large organizations. This is particularly likely if his organization's functions involve great uncertainty, rapidly changing environments [and] large expenditures.
>
> (Downs 1967: 71)

The phenomenon of means/ends reversal can result from specialization as different departments or divisions of the organization become so focused upon achieving their particular goals that they lose sight of the wider purpose of their activities. For example, if engineers are allowed an entirely free rein, the result may be 'state of the art' designs that promise to bankrupt the organization because they are commercially non-viable. Project TAURUS, a £500 million IT venture designed to streamline securities trading in the City of London, collapsed in 1993 while still under construction because the design had become so hopelessly complex that decision-makers were eventually forced to recognize that it might never work in the end. The project could have been stopped eighteen months earlier but project managers were so focused upon delivering the project that they failed to recognize that the project was no longer worth finishing and that it would be cheaper and simpler to start again. Instead their attention was absorbed in fixing one problem, only to discover that the result was to create a problem in another part of the system. A member of the group set up to monitor the project's construction explains what it was like:

> You'd say, 'How many of these issues have you resolved?' And they would say, 'We have resolved all of them.'
>
> And there was another page that was 'risks': 'What risks are you running?' There was a long list of risks ... every meeting they'd come with this chart and that chart and they would say, 'We have resolved all these issues, and now we have got another set of issues ... '
>
> So there was lots of progress. Every meeting lots of progress from where you were at the last meeting. However, when you sat back and said, 'Are we any closer to the end?'
>
> 'We-ll not really.'
>
> And that was really what was happening ... You knew people were working hard and they were getting work completed and putting it behind them and then they discovered there was this whole set of other things.
>
> (Drummond 1996: 113)

The result of means/ends reversal can be collective myopia. Another member of the monitoring group said:

> It's easy to look back and say, 'Why didn't you see it all the time?' Well, most disasters look obvious in hindsight. When you are in the middle of it and your objective is to get to the end you take each issue and you try to deal with it, and then another issue and you try to deal with it, and another issue and you try to deal with it.
>
> (Drummond 1996: 113)

How long do you go on dealing with it? Merton (1936) argues that it is precisely because habituated activity has previously led to goals attainment that it tends to become automatic. Actors may thus fail to realize that practices that have been successful in the past 'need not be so *under any and all conditions*' (Merton 1936: 901, italics in original).

Beyond rules

The existence of a comprehensive framework of rules is one of the defining features of bureaucracy. Yet organizations cannot legislate for every eventuality. What happens when the rules are silent or ambiguous? By definition then almost all rules are ambiguous as someone has to interpret them, and decide how to apply them and who they apply to (Weick 1979). Just as coroners must decide between 'death by suicide' and 'death by misadventure', rules become a set of instructions for generating difficulties that actors are required to solve (Brown 1978; see also Feldman 2000; Weick 1979):

> According to the coroner's instructions, the number of definitions they may use to define a dead body is limited. However, corpses do not come neatly labelled ... The coroner in doing his duty, finds convenient but non rational mechanisms for solving the problem of fitting recalcitrant cadavers into the limited categories of an organizational agenda.
>
> (Brown 1978: 370)

Just as roads were originally created by the routes that travellers took, rules do not so much guide action as emerge from action.

Moreover, the manner in which actors regularly solve problems becomes theory-in-action as distinct from espoused-theory. Although the former almost invariably bears some resemblance to the latter because of the limits imposed by the organizational agenda, the gap that develops between espoused-theory and what actual happens in practice may not be far from what was intended. Indeed, instead of regarding actors as rule bound it may be more accurate to think of them as forever making up their own rules (Weick 1979).

2 'A pisspot third-rate bank'

Barings merchant bank was founded on New Year's Day in 1763. Merchant bankers were originally merchants who used their good name to guarantee the trades of other merchants. For example, a trader in India might want to sell a cargo of spices to a merchant in London. If the seller merely accepted a bill of exchange from the buyer, it might prove worthless leaving the seller unpaid. In order to facilitate trade, smaller merchants paid a commission to respected merchants such as Barings to guarantee their bills (e.g. Wechsberg 1967).

Merchant bankers gradually ceased trading as merchants in order to concentrate upon the more profitable business of financing trade. By the early nineteenth century, Barings had become *the* leading house in international finance. Between 1793 and 1815 Barings took the lead role in raising £770 million in the London financial markets to finance war and imperial expansion, prompting the Duc de Richelieu to observe: 'There are six great powers in Europe: England, France, Prussia, Austria, Russia and Baring Brothers' (Ziegler 1988: 10).

As the century grew old Barings radiated an air of solidity and permanency:

> The partners' room ... was more like a gentleman's library with a cheerful open fire in a marble mantelpiece at the end of the room, and a soft red and blue rug. The mahogany desks were massive, and the chairs deeply upholstered in dark leather. In the centre of the room was a large table with a limited number of necessary reference books, and from the walls deceased partners of the House looked down from their mellow-gilt frames.
>
> (Kynaston 1994: 423)

This aura of comfort concealed a fault line. Barings had specialized in international finance, an occupation rather like investing in today's emerging markets involving a rollercoaster existence of not only high reward but also high risk. Moreover, since the mid-1880s Barings' senior partner Ned Baring (First Lord Revelstoke) had pursued a policy of investing heavily in Argentina, the nineteenth century equivalent of the modern day 'tiger economy' offering investors potentially huge returns on their capital. Revelstoke's enthusiasm for Argentina was shared by the general public. By the end of the decade British capital invested totalled more than £150 million (over £7 billion at today's levels) with Barings responsible for about a quarter of the sum advanced (Ziegler 1988).

In 1888, Revelstoke bought the much sought after concession for the Buenos Aires Water Supply and Drainage Company when it was sold by the Argentine government for $21 million in coined gold. In return for building the works, the contract gave Barings £10 million in shares and debentures in the company to sell to the general public. 'Since 1884 Messrs Baring have been growing bolder and bolder in their invitations to the public,' noted the *Statist* – the leading financial magazine of the day (Kynaston 1994: 423). Specifically in 1884 the amount raised was £6.5 million. In 1886 it was £10.25 million and in 1888 it was £28 million. The most successful of these was the Guinness flotation in 1886, a £6 million issue that attracted applications estimated at between £60 million and £120 million. When the flotation was announced, crowds of would-be investors besieged Barings' offices. The police were called to keep order as applicants resorted to wrapping their forms round stones and hurling them through Barings' windows in a desperate effort to acquire shares.

The waterworks issue was to be the boldest of them all. Normally when shares are sold to the public, the selling bank arranges for other banks to buy any unsold shares in return for a fee, a practice known as underwriting. Underwriting provides insurance in case the flotation turns out to be less popular than expected. Revelstoke was so confident that the waterworks issue would be an even bigger sell-out than the Guinness flotation that he decided to dispense with the expense of having the issue underwritten.

Indeed, Barings stood to reap a fortune from the venture – provided construction proceeded smoothly and provided the public bought the shares and debentures quickly. These were big provisos, however, and the venture soon went awry. Construction was hit by delays and costs escalated. Even more seriously the first stage of the flotation flopped. Barings had managed to sell less than a tenth of the £2 million of ordinary shares of the company. With large holdings in other South American securities locking up the firm's capital, Barings discovered itself in a position of appalling exposure: 'Up to the neck and rising' (Kynaston 1994: 426).

Unluckily for Barings the flotation coincided with a crisis of confidence in Argentine investments generally – a development akin to the collapse of markets in the Far East in 1998. Unwilling to signal failure by openly borrowing on the market, Revelstoke secretly negotiated loans from Glyns bank totalling £750,000 to provide temporary relief. A further crisis then erupted when the Argentine president resigned and the government threatened default. Such turbulence virtually ensured that no prospective investors would risk their capital in Argentina and that Barings would need to pay for the shares themselves.

Meanwhile, Revelstoke's son John Baring visited Argentina to see the situation. This was the first time Barings had any direct involvement in the venture – business previously having been conducted via an agent. John Baring discovered that the project was a shambles. There were no drawings, materials were inadequate, the works were overmanned and money was generally being squandered. Moreover, revenues were below target as many householders were either failing to use the service or using it without paying.

The final straw came when the Russian government withdrew £2 million of deposits from Barings. Revelstoke's brother Tom had been predicting disaster in Argentina for years. By November 1890 the market had realized that the partners were unable to identify the £9 million required to meet their obligations and the bank stood on the verge of collapse.

Barings was saved by the intervention of the Bank of England, which organized a guarantee fund financed by other leading banks and supported by the government. The partners were severely affected as their partnership was unlimited and they had to sell their estates, their town houses, paintings and other valuables to meet commitments to the guarantee fund. As the senior partner Revelstoke bore the largest proportion of the losses. Moreover, his career as a banker was now over as the old partnership was dissolved and a new one created. Revelstoke's losses were of little consolation to his partners.

> 'The name and the glory and the position and everything is gone,' wrote Tom Baring. 'Ned would have it all – glory and wealth. He might at least have guarded our good name. But it has all gone, offered up to his insatiate vanity and extravagance. I never thought I should have to write such a letter as this. Verily "A great Nemesis overtook Croesus". The line has never been out of my head since the Guinness success.'
>
> (Ziegler 1988: 252)

Revelstoke's catastrophic misjudgement taught the bank a lesson that would resonate down the years. Never again would Barings put its own capital at risk. From now on, Barings would eschew all forms of propriety trading, and content itself with earning a relatively modest living from fees and commissions charged to clients.

'A pisspot third-rate bank'

Just as the Victorian era lasted in the Sheffield steel industry until the 1960s, the same could be said for businesses practices in the City of London. In the 1960s while the United States was preparing to land astronauts on the moon, clerks still sat on high stools writing out cheques in long hand while the partners took dry sherry before lunch (Hobson 1991: 10). Business was conducted upon informal lines – even when huge sums of money were at stake. Formal methods of risk assessment were unheard of. Instead supplicants for credit were invited to lunch:

> One talks about everything except the matters one would really like to talk about – such as getting a million pound credit. The conversation is about farm- ing, roses, horses, politics, families ... The guest ... doesn't know all the time he is being scrutinised – his manners, his clothes, his speech, his sense (or lack) of humour, his attitude and personality. The general impression will decide whether he is going to be backed by a million pounds and whether any security will be demanded. This is the merchant banker's assessment – a mixture of

experience and flair, analysis and instinct ... Merchant banking is not a concrete science but an abstract art, and during lunch the practitioners of this art seem to work at their best. By the time the butler has served the traditional fruit cake and old port, there is usually unanimity in the minds of the partners about the risk – and about the client.

(Wechsberg 1967: 28)

The old City was seldom a magnet for the brightest or the best. The winds of change first began to blow shortly after the Second World War when the upstart Siegmund Warburg, a Jewish émigré, founded Warburg's bank. Warburg's habit of starting work at eight o'clock in the morning and his striving for meritocracy was considered contemptible by people in established houses (Reich 1980).

The most significant development, however, came in 1979 when the Conservative government under the premiership of Margaret Thatcher threatened to challenge the Stock Exchange's Rule Book in the Restrictive Practices court. An informal compromise was reached whereby the system of fixed commissions that protected smaller and less efficient firms was abolished. So too was single capacity where firms could be either brokers or jobbers, that is, either act as principals risking their own capital, or as intermediaries buying shares for clients but not both. In 1986 those developments crystallized into Big Bang (deregulation) and the dawning of a new and much more sharply competitive era as the City was opened up to foreign banks including huge integrated American investment banks like Morgan Stanley and Goldman Sachs.

Many old City partnerships sold out to the newcomers. Barings was among a handful of firms determined to try to preserve their independence in the post 'Big Bang' era. In the early 1980s Barings acquired a small stockbroking company known as Henderson-Crosthwaite. Stockbroking was attractive to Barings because (ever mindful of the 1890 debacle), it did not involve putting the bank's capital at risk. A broker merely acts as an intermediary buying or selling financial contracts on the instructions of a client and earns a living on the commission charged to the client.

In the early 1980s Barings employed about eight hundred people. The new acquisition employed only twenty, so Barings' directors perceived they would have little difficulty in controlling it. They also recognized that they would need to give their fledgling operation ample autonomy if it was to grow.

The experiment under the charismatic leadership of Christopher Heath proved highly successful. Within months Heath's firm had grown to seventy-five staff and in 1984 was renamed Barings Securities. Thereafter Barings enjoyed a virtual monopoly of access to the Japanese stock market and profited handsomely from it.

There were tensions, however. Brokers with their brightly coloured braces and loud ties tend to live for the day and are not interested in developing long term relationships with clients. By contrast Barings' merchant bankers lived in a relatively staid and gentlemanly world advising clients on corporate mergers and takeovers (Kynaston 2001). Part of the brokers' frustration was the continuing embargo upon propriety trading. Another centred upon status. Merchant bankers might see themselves as superior to mere brokers but increasingly it was the brokers who made money for Barings. In 1985 forecast profits for Barings Securities were £3.3 million. Actual profits far outstripped this estimate, totalling £10 million. In 1988 Barings the merchant bankers reported a £9 million loss, whereas Barings Securities made £60 million profit. As the brokers saw it, their efforts were paying the bonuses of a 'bunch of second-rate bankers from a "pisspot third-rate bank"' (Fay 1996: 33).

Relations between Barings' directors and Heath also became strained. Heath had discretion to report to Barings as he saw fit and Heath saw fit to report very little. Consequently Barings began to feel it was losing control over operations. Moreover, like many a charismatic leader, Heath was much more interested in generating new business than developing the administrative infrastructure needed to support it. If Heath wanted to open an office overseas he simply hired a hotel room and got started. Communication with staff was typically by word of mouth. Unproductive overheads including those associated with record keeping were kept to a minimum (Gapper and Denton 1996).

By 1991 Barings Securities employed 1100 people worldwide but only Heath and two close associates understood the financial structure in any depth (Gapper and Denton 1996). The crisis came in 1992 when Barings Securities made a loss. An inquiry was initiated. Barings' directors were horrified to discover that Heath not only had undertaken propriety trading without their knowledge and approval, but also had been borrowing money to finance it.

Barings' directors resolved to set Barings Securities in order. Heath resigned in March 1993 at the bank's request to make way for Peter Norris's appointment as Chief Executive (Gapper and Denton 1996). Norris's brief was to merge the two divisions in order to create a professionally managed organization with all the trappings of bureaucracy. The plan included bringing the two divisions under one roof in America Square, even though it meant moving out of 8 Bishopsgate – Barings' longstanding home. The merger was still being enacted when the bank collapsed.

Enter Nick Leeson

Nicholas William Leeson was born on 25 February 1967. His early life was spent in Watford, where his father worked as a plasterer and his mother worked as a nurse. Watford is a far cry from the so-called 'stockbroker belt' of Surrey where the partners of the former Henderson and Crosthwaite might have lived, as it houses many low-paid office workers based in London.

Leeson left school in 1985. His first job was settling cheques for the banking firm Coutts. Despite the prestige attached to the name of Coutts, Leeson found the job unbearably tedious. Two years later in 1987 he left Coutts to join Morgan Stanley as a trainee in the Settlements Division for Futures and Options. This was a more challenging role. Leeson learned a lot about the intricacies of back office work. The front office is where deals are struck and contracts traded. The back office settles transactions.

Leeson's real ambition was to be a trader. When he saw that Morgan Stanley offered no prospects in this direction, Leeson gave notice, even though he did not yet have another job to go to. He could afford to take the risk, because, as trading in exotic financial instruments expanded in the post 'Big Bang' era, experienced settlements staff were in high demand in the City.

On 10 July 1989 Leeson began working for Barings as a settlements clerk in the London back office. Settlement involves processing the paperwork associated with securities trading, for example, recording contract prices, reconciling customer payments to advances, and paying over collateral. Settlement is an important task but hardly a glamorous one. Consequently very few bank directors understand it in any detail, preferring to leave the intricacies of the task to salaried managers and employees.

Leeson worked hard at his new employment. He made such a good impression that he was seconded to Jakarta to deal with the backlog of work that had resulted from Barings Securities' energetic trading. Leeson says he was shocked by the contrast between the public image of Barings and the reality:

> When I read in Barings' glossy literature all about their innovative approach to doing business in the Far East, and how they had unique experience and a valuable customer base, I found that actually it was a complete mess ... Barings were sitting on £100 million worth of share certificates, which they couldn't pass on to the customers and claim the money because the certificates were in chaos. Nobody at Barings knew how to sort them out.
>
> (Leeson 1997: 35)

It took Leeson ten months to sort the mess out, working in an airless office in the sweltering heat. It was there that he met his future wife Lisa. The task duly completed, Leeson returned to London still nursing his ambition to become a trader:

> Every self-respecting clerk dreamed of becoming a trader, of putting on one of those grotesquely coloured jackets and shouting their heads off in the trading pit. They knew that this was the way to earn a fortune and buy a Porsche.
>
> (Leeson 1997: 29)

The licence application

In order to fulfil that ambition, Leeson needed a licence. Financial traders in the UK are licensed by the Financial Services Authority (FSA). In early 1992 Leeson asked Barings to apply on his behalf to the FSA for a licence to trade financial contracts. Although there were as yet no vacancies for traders within Barings, Leeson wanted to be eligible if an opportunity arose (Gapper and Denton 1996).

Barings applied in the usual way. The FSA's procedures involved a routine check of County Court records. The check revealed an unsatisfied debt of £639 (Board of Banking Supervision 1995). The debt related to an overdraft, and the

National Westminster Bank had obtained a court order against Leeson (Gapper and Denton 1996). Yet on his application form Leeson stated that he had no judgments against him.

On 10 March 1992, the FSA wrote to Barings' Company Secretary, notifying them of the discovery. Nine days later Barings decided to second Leeson to Singapore as a reward for his efforts in London and Jakarta. He left London shortly after the decision was announced. Meanwhile the FSA's letter lay in abeyance. In August 1992 the FSA wrote to Barings again asking whether it wished to pursue the application. This time Barings' newly appointed Head of Compliance, Valerie Thomas (who had previously worked for the FSA) replied, withdrawing the application (Board of Banking Supervision 1995).

Events in Singapore

Leeson was seconded to Singapore to set up and subsequently run the back office. His duties also involved managing local traders. In July 1992 Leeson applied to the Singapore Monetary Exchange (SIMEX) for a licence to trade in Singapore (Ministry for Finance, Singapore 1995). Leeson again made an incorrect statement on the application form, stating that he had not had any civil judgments entered against him. When SIMEX received the completed application form, it asked Barings to verify the information contained on the form. Without checking with London, the compliance office in Singapore confirmed that the information supplied by Leeson was correct. The licence was duly granted (Ministry for Finance, Singapore 1995).

Barings' Head of Compliance was based in London. From late 1992 onwards, she was assigned responsibility by Peter Norris for compliance on a global basis. Those responsibilities included acting as a focal point for all compliance issues. Barings also operated a system of local compliance officers reporting to local managers – in this case Simon Jones with a dotted line reporting relationship to London. In September 1993, Barings' Head of Compliance made a one-and-a-half day visit to Singapore. By this time Leeson was actively trading in his own right. The visit was prompted by the aforementioned expansion of the Head of Compliance's role to a global one. The Head of Compliance met with key local compliance staff and with SIMEX officials but did not mention the unsatisfied debt to SIMEX. This was followed by a one-and-a-half day visit to Singapore in March 1994. By then Leeson was emerging as Barings' star trader. Again no mention was made of the unsatisfied debt. In fact it was discovered only after the bank collapsed (Ministry for Finance, Singapore 1995: 52).

Compliance officers are also responsible for ensuring that records are properly kept. As we shall see later, this was an important issue in Singapore because Leeson ended up with responsibility for trading and settlement. In investment banks these two functions are normally segregated as a basic precaution against opportunism. Even though Leeson's roles were completely unsegregated, the compliance office in Singapore never checked his record keeping. Had they done so, their suspicions would almost certainly have been aroused. According to the

Head of Compliance, resource constraints precluded detailed examination of Leeson's records (Ministry for Finance, Singapore 1995: 53). There is no record of local staff petitioning London for additional resources or the Head of Compliance making a case for more staff in Singapore.

The audit report

Towards the end of 1994 the Head of Compliance received a copy of an internal audit report into Leeson's operations in Singapore. The report specifically said that Leeson's roles were completely unsegregated and that he was undertaking a mix of client and propriety trading. It is a matter of record that the Head of Compliance did not read the audit report – apparently because it did not explicitly call for action by compliance staff (Ministry for Finance, Singapore 1995: 51–54). It is unclear whether local compliance staff received a copy of the report. What is certain is that no one in the compliance offices of London or Singapore initiated any action in relation to it.

3   Failing most successfully

This book analyses how a small lapse in controls enabled Leeson to obtain a licence to trade despite being potentially ineligible. The main point of analysis concerns how actors may act in ways that are rational and rule-governed and yet their actions produce unwanted and unintended consequences. In order to do that it is first necessary to identify intention and then to specify what were the unanticipated and unwanted consequences arising directly from that action (further discussed in Merton 1936: 894–96).

In law a licence allows someone to do something that would otherwise be illegal. The intention of conducting background checks like the one initiated by the FSA is to protect the public interest. An important assumption in devising such checks is that people who do not observe high standards in their private lives may pose an unacceptable risk to the public and to organizations that employ them. At the very least, the information revealed by those checks can put organizations on their guard and if needs be prompt them to place restrictions upon an employee's freedom to operate.

Technically, a mechanism fails when expectations are not met (e.g. Bowen 1987). Ironically, the procedures initiated by the FSA were observed to the letter, and the mechanism for conducting background checks worked perfectly. The FSA did not just rely upon Leeson's word that he had no unsatisfied debts. It carried out an independent check, and the result of its inquiries contradicted information supplied by Leeson. When that discrepancy was discovered, the application was rightly referred back to Barings.

So far so good, but then the safeguard intended by the system failed. The discovery meant that Leeson was potentially ineligible to be licensed or might require conditions to be imposed upon his licence. However, it was not the unsatisfied debt that was the serious issue, but the possibility that Leeson tried to hide it. This was potentially a serious matter because in law an employee is expected to be honest towards their employer. Moreover, an employee should not bring their employer into disrepute by falsifying information to an outside body. Barings should have sought an explanation from Leeson. It is a matter of record that no investigation was made of the disclosure which raised a potential compliance issue.

Power refers to an actor's ability to achieve 'intended effects' (Wrong 1979, citing Bertrand Russell). In Leeson's case the background check failed to achieve the underlying 'intended effect' of preventing a potential opportunist from gaining access to the trading floor because the information revealed by the process was not followed up in an effective manner. The process of conducting background checks was part of the organization of power embodied in the wider compliance function. It was not power in itself, however. The process merely constituted the media through which power could be exercised (e.g. Clegg 1989) – or not. The trouble was the 'corpse' did not come neatly labelled. The fact that by now Leeson was virtually on his way to Singapore was irrelevant. Barings was entitled to an explanation, but seeking it required the exercise of initiative.

The FSA's subsequent letter to Barings was a chance to redeem the situation. At that pre-merger stage, Barings did not have a proper personnel department to give advice on how to conduct a disciplinary investigation. Even so, a key responsibility of the Head of Compliance (who answered the letter) was to ensure that only properly qualified and experienced persons were allowed to trade. So it was open to the Head of Compliance to act even though the rules did not actually require it.

The Head of Compliance subsequently said that the application was withdrawn because Leeson was already in Singapore (Ministry for Finance, Singapore 1995: 53). Another factor that may have influenced the decision to invoke the 'rules of irrelevance' (Brown 1989: ch. 7) was that Leeson had not gone to Singapore to be a trader but to be an office manager. The FSA's letter, moreover, asked only if Barings still wanted to pursue the application. It did not express any concern about the mis-statement or call for an investigation. It becomes an exercise in the tying up of administrative 'loose ends'. The FSA asks a question and duly receives an answer to that question – no more and no less. What occurs in this mechanistic exchange is that the rigid workings of bureaucracy ensure that the letter of the compliance is observed but not the spirit. A potential rogue trader thus slips through the minute crack between policy aimed at protecting the public interest and the gap created by the translation of that policy into a bureaucratic mechanism of control. It is a case of 'how to fail most successfully' (Watzlawick 1988).

Means/ends reversal

Leeson's second application offered a further line of defence. That failed because the background checks initiated by SIMEX relied upon information supplied by Barings and Barings' compliance staff in Singapore did not see fit to liaise with inquiries of their counterparts in London. It is unclear why this lapse occurred. Most likely it was because there was no system or procedure in place for making such checks and therefore staff took the easiest option and simply 'rubber stamped' the forms. At any rate what occurred was an extreme form of means/ends reversal (Drummond 1998b, 2001; Watson 1994) whereby the processing of the paperwork becomes an end in itself. The unintended and unwanted consequence that flows directly from this action is that the response sent by Barings to SIMEX was not worth the paper that it was written upon.

The impact of culture

What guides action in organizations when it comes to applying the rules in organizations, particularly when those rules are silent or ambiguous or where actors are presented with cases that do not fit neatly into the stipulated framework? What guides action when, as happened here, the audit report does not make explicit demands but nevertheless raises issues with implications for compliance? Why did doctors see nothing amiss in retaining (and sometimes displaying) specimens of human tissue without patients' knowledge or consent until a scandal erupted at Liverpool's Alder Hey hospital? Why did a routine and widespread practice suddenly become unacceptable?

A plausible possibility resides in notions of organizational culture. Organizations may be designed to function as machine-like bureaucracies but to see them as mere machines is to miss other important if less tangible aspects of organizational reality.

The word 'culture' is derived from the Latin, meaning to till the soil (Hofstede 1994). Within the organizational literature, culture has been defined as 'the way we do things round here' (Deal and Kennedy 1988) and 'why the organization is what it is' (Riley 1983: 437). The concept refers to the ideologies, customs, shared values, shared beliefs and shared understandings that inform action.

There are two views about the nature of culture. The post-modern view is that culture is something an organization *is* (Smircich 1983; see also Jelinek et al. 1983). A more conventional view is that culture is something an organization *has*. For example, in their celebrated work *In Search of Excellence*, Peters and Waterman (1982) turned the spotlight away from conventional mechanistic thinking and bureaucracy and instead emphasized the role of values, charisma and symbolism in sustaining the organization. Whatever we may feel about Peter and Waterman's work (for a particularly disturbing critique, see especially Willmott 1993; see also Ray 1986), it does serve as a reminder that organizations are not just governed by formal structural templates. Manipulating culture offers another way of exerting control.

This corporate culturism as it is sometimes called assumes that organizational effectiveness depends upon creating cultures that reflect the organization's mission (e.g. Deal and Kennedy 1988; Deming 1986; Pascale and Athos 1982; Peters and Waterman 1982; Wilkins and Ouchi 1983). Corporate culturism may explain, for example, why so few employees in Japan never take anywhere near their full holiday entitlement. It simply is not done. It may also explain the culture of long hours in the City whereby employees linger in offices till eight, nine, even ten o'clock at night, even though there is nothing for them to do. It is a subtle way of debarring women from employment in lucrative jobs without actually appearing to.

Culture may be reflected in organizational protocols and procedures – or lack of them. This point was graphically and tragically demonstrated on 18 November 1987, when a fire started under an escalator at King's Cross underground station. The fire brigade was summoned to deal with the blaze. As the heat intensified and black smoke engulfed the booking hall, Fire Station Officer Colin Townsley shouted reassuringly, 'It's all right love,' as he went to rescue a woman whose clothes were on fire:

> And then it happened. A massive fireball, generating temperatures of 1,200 C and more than six megawatts of energy exploded upwards consuming nearly four tonnes of material and incinerating thirty-one people in seconds.
>
> (Stern 1997: 156)

Station Officer Townsley was killed in the disaster.

Hitherto London Underground had enjoyed a good safety record, though there had been numerous fires in recent years including reports of passengers being led to safety through smoke-filled tunnels. A subsequent public inquiry concluded, however, that the disaster was caused by a deep-seated culture of complacency – possibly reinforced by a good formal safety record. Specifically:

> A belief that fires were inevitable, coupled with a belief that any fire on a wooden escalator, and there had been many, would never develop in a way that would harm passengers … That approach was seriously flawed for it failed to recognise the unpredictability of fire, that most unpredictable of all hazards. Moreover, it ignored the danger of smoke, which is almost certainly more deadly than fire.
>
> (Fennell 1988: 112)

This complacency culture was reflected in the less than robust operational procedures and training of London Underground staff. The station inspector who saw the fire in its early stages did not know how to use emergency equipment. A clerk in the ticket office went to inspect the blaze and then returned to his office because he saw it as no part of his duties to act. No one alerted staff of the Bureau de Change and other shops adjacent to the booking hall of the danger. Trains from the Northern Line continued disgorging passengers onto the platform at King's Cross as late as 19:48, that is, three minutes after the flashover had occurred.

Culture can also take over where formal protocols leave off. Indeed, culture can be seen as representing the last line of control in organizations (see especially Ray 1986). Although critical theorists like Ray view cultural control as a potentially sinister move to drive down the transaction costs of relying upon bureaucratic mechanisms of surveillance, conceivably a well-developed system of shared values can ensure actors respond in an appropriate manner where the rules are no longer helpful.

While we cannot 'prove' the existence of a culture, we can infer something about shared values from how actors behave. The practice of organ retention spoke volumes about where patients really stood in clinicians' eyes. By the same token Leeson (1996: 86) says that many of Barings' practices would have been 'unthinkable' in Morgan Stanley, that is, in an organization more culturally attuned to the risks involved in trading financial contracts. We can infer from Leeson's observation that in a more disciplined culture, the referral from the FSA would have been investigated. In contrast, there was nothing in Barings' culture to prompt compliance staff to be proactive.

The psychology of loss

The two visits made by the Head of Compliance to Singapore offered a further line of defence. According to the Head of Compliance, the purpose of those visits was not to become enmeshed in detail, but to meet local staff and ensure that the requisite systems and procedures were in place (Ministry for Finance, Singapore 1995: 51–54). Even so, she could have asked how Leeson had managed to obtain a licence to trade and asked to see his application form. Had she done so, her investigation would have revealed that existing systems and procedures left something to be desired.

Although managers in bureaucracies almost inevitably accumulate 'skeletons' in cupboards (Downs 1967), that does not always mean they have to stay there. Any suggestion as to why the Head of Compliance allowed this particular 'skeleton' to reside in the cupboard must be speculative. Prospect theory offers a plausible explanation. In essence the theory suggests that faced with a choice between accepting a definite loss and the possibility of avoiding that loss altogether, but at the risk of subsequently incurring a much greater one, most of us would prefer to avoid a definite loss (Kahneman and Tversky 1979; see also Banaji et al. 2003; Bazerman 2005; Bazerman et al. 1997; Bazerman et al. 2006). To have intervened in Leeson's trading in 1994, and even in 1993, not only would have meant admitting mistakes had been made, but also would have meant incurring disapprobation for upsetting Barings' nascent star trader. On the other hand, at that time it would have seemed highly unlikely that the skeleton would ever tumble out of the cupboard. In other words, to mix metaphors, if the Head of Compliance did confront her options, there would have been a powerful psychological driver for letting sleeping dogs lie.

Control as form

Even so, such passivity raises another question, namely what were all those compliance staff doing there? They were certainly not distracted by the audit report, because no one read it. Nor were local compliance staff absorbed in checking Leeson's record keeping – or even as much as conducting a superficial examination. The FSA too was at fault for not demanding action from Barings. What is the point of a licensing system that ignores a fundamental question of probity?

What indeed? Recall that the trope irony highlights the paradox of the unexpected and the inevitable. Conceivably Leeson obtained a licence and, as we shall see later in this book, subsequently behaved with impunity not so much despite the existence of a compliance function but rather *because* of it. More specifically, whereas conventional mechanistic views of organization assign concrete meaning to organizational artefacts, the literature on symbols and symbolic action in organizations (known as the metaphor of text) suggests that the organization can be read as if it were a symbolic document. It is the difference between what Merton (1936) calls the ostensible and latent function of organizational activity. For example, ostensibly office furniture serves an instrumental function, but it can also be 'read' as conveying a latent message about the status of the user.

The literature on organizational symbolism is problematic because, like culture, it addresses the intangible aspects of organizational life. For our purposes a symbol can be defined as a 'sign which denotes something much greater than itself, and which calls for the association of certain conscious or unconscious ideas in order for it to be endowed with its full meaning and significance' (Morgan et al. 1983: 5).

All symbols are signs but not all signs are symbols. For something to be a symbol, it must be vested with a deeper level of meaning than surface appearances might suggest. For example, the lighting of a candle may serve an instrumental purpose by illuminating a room. The gesture may also be symbolically significant if it denotes relief from suffering or the bringing of enlightenment. Likewise, in a riot it is often the police officer's helmet that ends up being kicked along the pavement because in addition to its instrumental function of providing protective headgear, it is also a symbol of power and authority.

Symbols can play a useful role in maintaining social systems (Dandridge et al. 1980). For instance, Barley (1983) observed how morticians avoid having their work disrupted by grieving relations by making everything associated with death appear as lifelike as possible – closing the eyes of the corpse to give the appearance of sleep, tidying the room in which the person has died and so forth. If symbols can impart the appearance of life to something as final as death (Jelinek et al. 1983), just what is the extent of their power?

That question is beyond the scope of this book. Suffice be it here to note that in an influential article, Meyer and Rowan (1978) argued that perceived legitimacy is a more important factor in organizational survival than instrumental efficiency (see also Edelman 1971; Pfeffer 1981; Uzzi 1999, 1997). For example, Arnold and Sikka (2001) argue that the Bank of England had long entertained serious doubts about the probity of BCCI but intervened only when the bank's activities threatened to undermine the legitimacy of the banking system as a whole. Likewise, organizations sacrifice some immediate economic benefit by adopting 'green' policies and selling Fairtrade goods in order to enhance their legitimacy and thus guarantee their long term survival.

In a similar vein Pfeffer (1981) has argued that the trappings of organization are frequently retained more for their symbolic role in enhancing perceived legitimacy than for their instrumental value to the organization. For example, says Pfeffer, consultation processes seldom genuinely seek to solicit employees' views but aimed at creating a sense of involvement in order that the signal of increased attention and importance may energize and motivate organizational participants. Likewise, organizations embody strategic planning, yet what is planning if not 'dreaming with discipline' (Brown 1989: ch. 7). Planning is symbolically important because it abolishes the unpredictable future. To paraphrase Brown (1989), planning soothes our fears for the future in much the same way as psychoanalysis deals with our fears of the past. Like the activities of morticians, symbolically planning transforms reality because it imparts an air of control and certainty where little exists.

The same goes for the trappings of management. Arguably the panoply of clinical governance, risk management and safety inspections exists to cloak organizations and institutions in an air of respectability, thereby guaranteeing their legitimacy. Pfeffer (1981), for example, argues that the satisfaction of demands by creating a regulatory body like the FSA may convince people that action has been taken to control and monitor organizational activities. As we saw here, the reality may be different. Likewise, for all the rhetoric surrounding clinical governance and all the elaborate systems and procedures involved, the fact remains that whereas airline pilots can expect to be tested at least 100 times during their working lives, at the time of writing doctors can proceed from initially qualifying through to retirement without ever having their competence revalidated, even though research has shown that clinical judgement deteriorates with age (Chief Medical Officer 2006: xi–xii).

Licensing procedures, background checks and management speak like 'ensuring systems and procedures are in place' and indeed audit (see Power 1997) represent rituals of verification and reassurance. To be more precise, according to the *Oxford Concise Dictionary*, rite means 'form' of procedure, action required,' and ritual refers to 'prescribed order of performing … rites'. Rituals are more important for what they signify than what they actually do (Pettigrew 1979). The appointment of a new leader can be highly ritualistic. A great fuss is made as special selection committees are convened, elaborate programmes of visits, presentations and interviews are arranged and so forth. The ritual is expensive and time consuming but it emphasizes the special skills allegedly involved in leadership and the objectivity of the recruitment process (Pfeffer 1977).

The activities undertaken by compliance staff can be seen in the same light. That is, when the 'rubber stamp' is applied, check boxes ticked and so forth, the ritual is observed and everyone is satisfied. Ostensibly systems of governance, like the compliance function, exist to make organizations safe. In reality they may lull us into a false sense of security by making us think we are safe.

4 The dynamics of power

A famous *Punch* cartoon depicts two Daleks at the foot of a flight of stairs. The caption reads, 'This certainly buggers our plans to conquer the universe.' The moral of the story is that a mighty power can be thwarted by something as mundane as a flight of stairs.

In fact, no form of power is absolute, despite what appearances may suggest. No matter how asymmetrical the relationship between controller and controlled, the weaker party always has some leverage (discussed further in Wrong 1979). The Nazis discovered this to their cost when they tried to set up administrative control of occupied countries. Here was an extreme case of power imbalance between ruler and ruled. Moreover the Nazis were supported by a huge arsenal of negative sanctions and had no moral scruples that would restrain them from using them against resistant subjects. Time and again their directives were thwarted. Yet no one was ever called to account for disobeying orders because there was no disobedience – or if there was, it was very subtle. Rather the Nazis were undermined by the 'normal' workings of bureaucracy:

> A directive from the top may have to be transferred and translated (reformulated, elaborated, operationalized) several times before it reaches its destination and becomes implemented. Such processes of transmission obviously provide some scope for detaining, deflecting, or diluting 'from below' the commands or decrees from 'above'.
>
> (Lammers 1988: 439)

The power to detain, deflect, dilute or otherwise undermine one's hierarchical superiors arises from the organization's dependency upon employees as agents to execute directives and uphold values. Such dependency invariably offers a measure of autonomy and with it the option of acting differently from what the organization intends (e.g. Giddens 1979; Mechanic 1962). Although conventional wisdom asserts that 'to rule is to serve', the Tao recognizes the potentially subtle nature of resistance as it says 'to serve is to rule' (e.g. Wing 1988).

The ability to exert control while in a subordinate role arises in part because employees have access to resources, namely people, instrumentalities and information, that can be used for unintended purposes (Mechanic 1962). Mechanic (1962) suggests that informal power becomes enhanced where a lower participant controls something of importance to the organization. For example, lowly clerks entrusted with the task of photocopying important documents may end up better informed about the organization than their hierarchical superiors.

Another important factor is the intensity of control. Actors at the higher echelons typically enjoy a wide scope of power. That is, they control many things but because they are spread so thinly and have so many matters calling for their attention, it is bound to be control with a light touch. Conversely, actors at the lower echelons may not control many things but because of the narrow scope of their power they may be able to exert intense control (further discussed in Wrong 1979). Such control may reach a level of intensity such that it becomes impenetrable to an outsider. For example, the administration of the ancient Chinese empire was undermined to a colossal extent thanks to clerks and their resort to:

> Deceit, obfuscation, chicanery, collusion, and the selective performance of assigned tasks and partly due to their mastery over administrative detail and operating procedure, these low ranking subordinates were able to confound, frustrate, inveigle and even intimidate their more prestigious superiors.
>
> (Sterba 1978: 70)

Higher officials in the Chinese civil service tried for 1300 years to bring the recalcitrant clerks under control! A more modern parallel resides in Pettigrew's (1972) fictional character Kenny, who used his control over information and strategic position as 'gatekeeper' in the organization to exert decisive influence over the choice of computer supplier.

Organization dynamics

Access to resources alone cannot explain informal power because resources are not in themselves power. They are only the media through which power may be exercised (Clegg 1989; Giddens 1979). As Clegg (1989) points out, virtually anything can be turned into a resource. Moreover, Mechanic (1962) assumes that a clear and definite distinction exists between formal and informal power. While this may be true in theory, in practice the distinction may be problematic because power is an inherently dynamic entity. For example, Dalton (1959) has argued:

> Multiple relations, with continuous interaction and change, become too dynamic to be handled entirely inside such conceptual walls as 'formal-informal' ... Exclusive reliance on this couplet ignores the whole-confused middle ground where there are 'mixtures' and where new formal and informal actions are obscurely initiated.
>
> (Dalton 1959: 222)

Giddens (1979, 1984) goes further than Dalton, as he suggests that while power in organizations is embodied in structure as depicted, for example, in job descriptions and organization charts, the 'living breathing' organization is far from static as organizational actors by their actions are constantly creating and recreating structure.

We shall pursue Giddens' ideas on structure later in this book. Here it is sufficient to note that even the lowliest actor can have an impact when it comes to shaping the organization. The question to be explored here is how do actors create and recreate structure? Hatch (1999) suggests that actors can influence what happens by seeing their structures not as written in 'tablets of stone' but as freehand sketches. Just as in improvisational jazz, players not only follow the tune being played but also influence the tune by experimenting with tonality, tempo and so forth, organizational actors take their cue both from the notes on the page (structure) and from another.

Such flexibility is enabled by the inherently ambiguous nature of structure. Whereas bureaucratic models of organization either assume that organizational existence is either unambiguous, or, that ambiguity is a temporary state of affairs awaiting correction, Hatch (1999) argues structure is inherently ambiguous, and that ambiguity presents the 'empty space' whereby actors can insert their own ideas about what should be done. Moreover, instead of seeing actors as confined within boundaries, Hatch (1999) suggests that it is more realistic to imagine actors as forever testing boundaries. That is, like improvisational jazz players, actors are continuously pushing limits, quite literally seeing what they can get away with.

The colourful imagery of improvisational jazz can be misleading in that it depicts organizations as existing almost on the verge of anarchy. According to Feldman (2000), however, no special knowledge or access may be required in order to effect a transformation. Feldman argues that organizations may be changed simply by actors following their routines. Routines, to paraphrase Feldman (2000), refer to structural templates (rules) that actors use in order to accomplish their daily work, namely, '*Repeated patterns of behaviour that are bound by rules and customs and that do not change very much from one iteration to another*' (Feldman 2000: 611, italics in original).

In other words, according to Feldman, even when actors conscientiously attempt to follow the official line, that is, play the notes as they appear on the score, they may effect profound change. Intuitively we might think that the enactment of routines 'by the book' will guarantee uniform outcomes. According to Feldman this assumption is not always borne out in practice. This is because there are three factors in the equation, namely the agent, the routines and the outcomes, all inter-acting with one another in ways that may be difficult to predict, far less control:

> One can think of routines as flows of interconnected ideas, actions and outcomes. Ideas produce actions, actions produce outcomes and outcomes produce new ideas. It is the relationship between these elements that generates change.
>
> (Feldman 2000: 613)

Clearly there are limits on the freedoms that employees enjoy to translate ideas into actions. For example, when it comes to IT and information systems, organizations tend to be designed with very clear rules and restrictions in order to prevent employees abusing power (e.g. Laudon and Laudon 1999). For example, passwords are used to limit access, usage of the facility is monitored as a second line of defence and 'what's on the system' may be periodically audited as a further line of defence.

Yet IT professionals also recognize that too many controls can be cumbersome and may discourage employees from using the system and lead to organizational inefficiency. In addition, it is difficult if not impossible for organizations to monitor every aspect of a system's usage. For that reason risk analysis is sometimes used to strike a balance between the organization's need for control and the organization's need for flexibility. Generally speaking more sensitive information is subject to greater protection and monitoring than information that is perceived as routine and low level.

Feldman (2000) argues that we should not place too much confidence in such rational approaches to control because of the uncontrollable element. Like Perrow (1984), Feldman argues that a change in one part of a system conceived and designed on rational principles can trigger unpredictable variation in another part and so on until the sum total of variations results in catastrophe. The difference between the two authors is that whereas Perrow was thinking of disasters at safety critical sites like Three Mile Island (and subsequently Chernobyl and Bhopal), Feldman's thesis is that the mundane features of organizations like day-to-day office work can also produce unpredictable variation:

> The fit between the ideas, actions and outcomes is not always tight. Ideas can generate actions that do not, in fact, execute the ideas. Actions can generate outcomes that make new and different actions possible or necessary. *The outcome could for instance be a disaster* ...
>
> (Feldman 2000: 613, italics added)

On that note, let us now return to events in Barings.

5 Did Nick Leeson have an accomplice?

In 1992 the Singapore Monetary Exchange (SIMEX) was a relative newcomer to the financial markets. Keen to attract business, SIMEX rules were much more customer friendly than those operated by longer established exchanges in the Far East, and dealing fees cheaper. Another of Leeson's duties involved executing trades for colleagues based in Japan acting for customers wishing to take advantage of the facilities offered by SIMEX.

In theory executing trades is a straightforward task. Leeson was simply required to sit by a telephone and take telephone orders to buy or sell financial contracts at a given price and then repair to the floor of the exchange to conduct the transaction. In practice it is not quite as easy as it sounds. For example, in the noise and tumult of the trading pit a contract to buy might easily be wrongly executed as a contract to sell. It is normal practice in investment banking that when a mistake occurs, the customer is made good and the bank stands the loss, which is booked to an error account.

Leeson made a lot of errors while mastering execution. He hid the resultant losses in a secret account number 88888 – known as the 'five-eights' account. According to Leeson his misuse of account 88888 started in October 1992, when an inexperienced employee made a mistake that initially cost Barings £20,000. Simon Jones instructed Leeson to inform Andrew Baylis in London and to sack the unfortunate employee, who in fact never returned to Barings. Leeson hesitated to inform Baylis. Meanwhile the loss escalated to £60,000 because of adverse market movement. Although Leeson's recollection is incorrect in that the misuse of account 88888 actually began in July 1992, an error of this magnitude posed a new problem:

> £60,000 was far too big a figure to tell Simon Jones. And now I also had the problem of explaining why I hadn't told anyone all week. So I pushed the £60,000 under the carpet and into the 88888 account. If I told Simon Jones … [he] might … slam me back down into Settlements.
>
> (Leeson 1997: 62)

Thereafter Leeson's use of the five-eights account became habitual such that by the end of 1992 it contained over thirty large errors: 'This was bad but not catastrophic.

There were other errors in the London account, but I put into 88888 the particularly large discrepancies ... There was no hard and fast rule – an error's an error' (Leeson 1997: 63).

'Shooting fish in a barrel'

Meanwhile his colleagues in Japan saw something rather different and altogether more promising. Leeson seemed to have a magical ability to obtain prices below market rates. Indeed he became so successful that Barings began charging customers a premium for his execution services. In fact, Leeson was deliberately underpricing business in order to ingratiate himself with colleagues in Japan. Those losses were also hidden in the five-eights account.

By September 1992 the losses had become too great for them to be kept hidden indefinitely, prompting Leeson to try to trade his way back into profit. Since Leeson had no authority to risk Barings' capital, he told Barings that he had discovered an opportunity to generate 'risk-free' profits from arbitrage. For example, if oranges cost 10p in London and 11p in Dublin, the arbitrageur buys a quantity of oranges in London and immediately sells them on in Dublin. Arbitrage does not involve predicting market movements as the arbitrageur merely exploits price anomalies between markets. Provided a contract to buy is matched with a contract to sell, the only risk is one of market movement in the time it takes for contracts to be executed. Barings therefore deemed arbitrage to be an activity that was 'essentially without risk' (Secretary of State versus Tuckey) or to paraphrase Gapper and Denton (1996: 10), like 'shooting fish in a barrel'.

In practice, arbitrage in financial markets is more difficult than it sounds because price differentials are both wafer thin and fleeting – as several of Leeson's colleagues in Japan had discovered, having tried their hand at it and lost money. Leeson's situation was apparently different, however. According to Leeson, whenever options are bought or sold in significant quantities, there is a domino effect in the market. As Barings understood it, Leeson's knowledge of customers' orders enabled him to anticipate the emergence of price differentials and arbitrage profitably, a practice known as 'front running' a customer, or insider trading in other words.

In fact Leeson was not conducting arbitrage at all, but selling options. An option gives another party the right, but not the obligation, to buy or sell a given quantity at some date in the future in return for payment of a premium, for example, to buy 1000 oranges at 10p each in nine months' time. If at the end of nine months the price of oranges has fallen to 9p, the option expires worthless. However, if the price of oranges has risen to 11p, the option is exercised. Options trading is extremely risky because the party granting the option is obliged to supply the oranges at the contracted price regardless of how far the market may have moved in the mean time. If the price of oranges rises say to 20p or more, the loss may far outstrip the premium received for granting the option (Gapper and Denton 1996: 24).

The options sold by Leeson were contracts known as straddles, that is, double contracts which would lose money if the market fell or rose in value when the option expired six or even nine months hence. The only way the seller made money was if the market remained completely stable. If that happened the seller could retain the premium – a remote contingency, however, given the timescales involved. The attraction to Leeson was that he gained two lots of premium meanwhile (for a more detailed and technically sophisticated account of Leeson's trading, see Stonham 1996a, 1996b).

Options are mainly bought as insurance against currency fluctuations. Leeson was forbidden to expose Barings to such risk but he could buy and sell for Barings' customers. That was precisely what Leeson was doing, only the customer was Barings.

Account 88888

Let us now backtrack and consider precisely how Leeson managed to conceal his unauthorized trades. Barings' CONTAC system would send details of 99905 (the original error account that listed Leeson's initial mistakes) to London and details of thirty-six other accounts every day. On 3 July 1992, Leeson's line manager in London Gordon Bowser telephoned Leeson to say he did not want all the details of 99905 because they were causing reconciliation problems. Specifically, the small errors had become so numerous that they were undermining the First Futures IT system. Leeson agreed to set up another account to hold minor errors:

> Bowser: 'Can you set up another Error Account and keep them all in Singapore? We don't want to be bothered with all these tiny errors you're clocking up. There's over fifty a day, and so there are a hundred entries needed to reverse them. The auditors will start asking questions.'
>
> I put the phone down and turned to Risselle.
>
> 'Can you create another file?' I asked her. 'We need another Error Account.'
>
> 'Sure,' she said, clearing her screen and tapping keys. 'It's all ready. What number do you want to give it?'
>
> (Leeson 1997: 53)

Leeson recounts that he asked the clerk to suggest a lucky number. The clerk told Leeson that eight is a very lucky Chinese number. Leeson replied:

> 'How many numbers does it have to be?'
>
> 'Five.'
>
> '… Let's give it all the luck it can handle. Let's call it 88888.'
>
> (Leeson 1997: 53)

Leeson then instructed a software engineer to amend the reporting software to exclude the five-eights account from the daily feed to London.

Approximately three weeks later Bowser telephoned Leeson and reversed the instruction as the IT system had been upgraded to handle small errors. Leeson duly complied and small trading errors were once again reported to London. In consequence the five-eights account was now a dormant account. It was still lodged in the computer, however.

Leeson began to use this account to conceal the losses made on underpriced contracts and later to hide unauthorized options trading. When these trades were fed into the SIMEX computer system, Leeson originally designated them as house trades. In other words, the designation of the account suggested that the transactions (and accompanying market risk) were booked to Barings. On 17 July, Leeson filled in a form redesignating the account as client trades. This was significant because it suggested that any exposure to risk was a client rather than Barings. By late August 1992, account 88888 contained so many trades that it became a reportable account under SIMEX rules. Accordingly on 26 August 1992, Leeson faxed a BC4 form to SIMEX which identified the account as 'Baring Securities London – Error Account' and described it as a Related House Account. That same day, Leeson faxed an amended BC4 form to supersede the previous submission. It was identical to the previous form except that the reference to the account being an 'Error Account' was removed.

Thereafter the volumes of transactions booked to the five-eights account rose from 189 in July 1992 to approximately 7000 by January 1995 yet that was only a fraction of the final total. By 24 February 1995 there were over 61,000 contracts concealed in the accounts. SIMEX did not become suspicious at the volume and value of transactions listed because it appeared to be a bona fide customer account.

The stage was now set for Leeson to sell options without authority and to use the premium received to cover his losses. Options trading is not only risky; but also requires a mathematician to calculate the premium necessary to offset the risk. Lacking the necessary mathematical sophistication, Leeson sold too cheaply and became trapped in an escalatory spiral writing more and more options in increasingly desperate efforts to recoup his losses. Since the premium received was booked as pure profit, the more money Leeson lost the more profitable his trading apparently became while in reality Barings was exposed to huge risk.

An opportunity lost

Yet Barings' financial controllers in London did know about the five-eights account, albeit indirectly. Although the listings of contracts were not transmitted to London, a file was posted to London which made reference to account 88888 but either it was not noticed or its significance was not appreciated.

The system worked as follows. Information was received from Singapore to be entered onto the so-called First Futures system in London. First Futures first checked whether it recognized the account number by making reference to a master file, which contained a list of all known account numbers. Since the number 88888 did not appear on the master list, the data was rejected by the First Futures system. In consequence the information was not downloaded into the

First Futures system. There was therefore nothing in the ledger referring to the five-eights account.

The information concerning account 88888 was left in a suspense file. Moreover, the system did not detail which accounts had been skipped during the downloading process. The Head of IT at Barings subsequently told the Board of Banking Supervision that there were two 'margin processing' screens available to users of the First Futures system. The first screen listed all the margin balances loaded from the CONTAC system in Singapore. The second screen listed the accounts recognized by First Futures as being valid London accounts, for which the margin balances were loaded into the First Futures database. If the two screens had been compared, it would have been clear which accounts were being rejected by First Futures as irrelevant.

It is a matter of record that this comparison was never made. Moreover, there were no system based reconciliations or control totals to ensure that records received in London were examined. Unreconciled accounts would be held in suspense to await allocation. The settlement staffs in London were responsible for clearing out suspense files. Barings' Head of Settlements subsequently told the Board of Banking Supervision that she never saw account 88888 and discovered the account in the margin file only after Barings had collapsed along with a suite of other accounts that did not belong to Barings. She had no idea how long it had been there. Had all the accounts from Singapore been printed off, questions might have been asked. However, the Head of Settlements did not regard it as her or her department's responsibility to undertake the task.

Although in Chinese superstition eight is regarded as lucky because it means 'to prosper', five is seen as highly unlucky because it means 'never'. Shortly after Leeson mysteriously disappeared, his colleagues discovered the printout of the five-eights account lying on his desk. Every one of the 61,000 contracts listed in the 'never prosper' account was losing money.

6 Analysing the fatal disconnect

The striking feature of the story of the 'never prosper' account is the contrast between the mundane acts whereby the account was created and the catastrophic consequences that followed. Again the system of bureaucratic surveillance did not fail but worked almost exactly as it was intended to. Yet malfeasance on a large scale went undetected for nearly three years, despite the existence of computer generated management information pointing directly to it. Moreover, Barings was destroyed not by the malevolent genius of a computer 'hacker' or technically literate insider. It took just a few strokes on a computer keyboard and some routine form filling to set the stage for Barings' destruction.

Analysis seeks to answer two questions:

- How was Leeson able to evade organizational controls in order to establish the account?
- Why did the existence of the account go unnoticed until after Barings collapsed?

Recall, in theory opportunism in organizations is virtually impossible because organizations employ bureaucratic techniques of surveillance including IT systems in order to ensure that employees observe their contractual obligations (Ouchi 1980; Williamson 1975, 1981, 1991). In practice, perfect control is impossible to achieve. This is because organizations rely upon employees as agents to execute their directives. Such dependence invariably confers some autonomy, that is, the option of acting differently from what the organization intends (e.g. Giddens 1979; Wrong 1979). Barings depended upon Leeson to execute trades. In order to counterbalance such dependency and to discourage opportunism, there is an elaborate system of surveillance where the idea is that all errors are reported to London. In theory controllers in London know about every transaction in Singapore. Thus does information technology enable Barings to operate remote outposts as it transcends the distance in time and space.

The Icarus paradox

The control system in other words reflected linear intuitive thinking that 'more is better'. In this view, more monitoring means more control. Yet nothing goes on getting better indefinitely, otherwise trees would touch the skies. Indeed, we can get too much of a good thing. In Greek mythology the fabled Icarus acquired wings made of wax that enabled him to fly. Icarus used his newfound capability to fly higher and higher and eventually got so close to the sun that his wings melted, sending him plunging to his death in the Aegean Sea. The moral of the so-called Icarus paradox is that it may be the very things that make us successful that ultimately destroy us. For example, firms that become successful through taking calculated risks may eventually succumb to recklessness. Conversely firms that have prospered through cautious expansion may become moribund through failing to make necessary changes (further discussed in Miller 1992).

Barings made a similar discovery to its cost. Just as there were limits to how high the fabled Icarus could safely fly, there are limits to what software can safely handle. Control negates control as the profusion of errors reported by Leeson undermines the reconciliation process. In order to address this unforeseen and unwanted outcome, Barings tells Leeson to stop reporting small errors. The idea is that it is necessary to sacrifice some control over matters of detail in order to re-establish overarching control. Eventually the software is amended so that the original idea of total control can be reimposed.

Leeson complies with the instruction to stop reporting small errors and duly sets up a separate error account. Although Leeson's misuse of the account did not begin immediately, the action of setting it up seems to have resulted in the germ of an idea as he gives it a special number.

Authority exists where one party has an acknowledged right to command and another party perceives an obligation to obey. Authority differs from power in that power is the ability to achieve one's ends regardless of whether one has authority (e.g. Wrong 1979). Leeson was clearly authorized to set up a new account and, initially, to withhold details of the account from London. By exercising his legitimate authority in a more or less legitimate manner, Leeson effectively *re*formed the organizational structure in a small way.

When London eventually reasserts control by instructing Leeson to resume reporting all errors, the outcome is a slight and yet crucial disconnect in the flow between ideas, actions and outcomes (Feldman 2000), as Leeson now has a dormant account outside reporting systems. Moreover, like the clerks of the ancient Chinese civil service, the sheer intensity of his power over this crucial instrumentality meant that he could keep it a secret. The disciplinary gaze of surveillance systems might be far reaching, but they would never discover the account's existence. Thus do bureaucratic controls designed to limit opportunism give rise to it (Merton 1936, 1948, 1957; see also Cameron and Quinn 1988).

Had Leeson not been bent on chicanery, obfuscation and deceit, it might not have mattered. After all, dormant accounts are hardly unusual in organizations. What ultimately mattered was the use Leeson made of the account. Structure may be inherently ambiguous and employees may have considerable discretion when it comes to applying the rules (e.g. Brown 1978; Giddens 1979; Hatch 1999), 'an error's an error'. What is clear, however, is that Leeson had no authority whatsoever to use the five-eights account to store unauthorized trades.

There was one further task for Leeson to accomplish. The system of registering accounts was part of SIMEX's system of monitoring trading in order to ensure that firms like Barings complied with the rules, and to ensure that the correct amount of margin was called when due. The system has one flaw, however, and that is it relies upon information supplied by member organizations. Leeson uses his mastery over procedure and access to the forms to redesignate the account on SIMEX records. SIMEX accepted the change without question. Indeed, it had no reason to question the changes because account 88888 was being used as a customer account so this slight but important change in routine attracts neither attention nor comment. Acceptance of the form is a 'normal' programmed decision. Yet the predicted flow between ideas, actions and outcomes breaks down as Leeson again manipulates controls in order to evade control. It was an error account and therefore strictly speaking a house account (see also Chapter 8). It is now a customer account. The chicanery that SIMEX is not aware of is the identity of the customer. Therein lies another disconnect between theory and practice.

The parable of the drunkard

All was not lost. The outcroppings of malfeasance have a habit of showing up somewhere in the organization. Leeson seems to have been unaware that data pertaining to account 88888 was being posted to London. It is unclear why the suspense file was not audited during the three years or so that Leeson was operating account 88888. A plausible possibility is that the suspense file was ignored precisely because of the disconnection between ideas, actions and outcomes. In more colloquial language the suspense account became a dustbin for all the 'rubbish' generated by 'the system'. One can imagine staff in Barings talking about the account: 'God knows what's in there! The system's throwing up accounts that don't even belong to us!' Conceivably what may have occurred is an example of the 'paradox of consequences' whereby organizations prefer to exercise control and surveillance by focusing upon what is easy. It is like the drunkard who searches for the car keys not where he dropped them but under the lamp post because the light is good (Watzlawick et al. 1974).

7 Agency, structure and organizational collapse

> I don't know what effect these men will have on the enemy, but by God they frighten me.
>
> (Duke of Wellington)

> One afternoon at Khe Sanh a Marine opened the door of a latrine and was killed by a grenade that had been rigged upon the door. The Command tried to blame it on a North Vietnamese infiltrator, but the grunts knew what had happened: 'Like a gook is really gonna tunnel all the way here to booby-trap a shithouse, right? Some guy just flipped out is all.'
>
> (*Dispatches*, Herr 1977: 56)

As this disturbing quotation from Michael Herr's account of soldiers in Vietnam shows, strange things can happen in organizations. While it would be wrong to suggest Leeson destroyed Barings single-handed, he nevertheless played a highly significant role in events. Having analysed how Leeson used technology to set the stage for his unauthorized trading, attention now shifts to Leeson's early days in Barings and his relationships with other key actors.

More specifically, the exploration concerns the period between March 1992 and end of December 1994 and the transition from Leeson's role as mere order filler to his emergence as Barings' star trader. In order to provide a conceptual lens for this examination, it is necessary to continue with the themes of lower participant power and organization structure and in particular how actors can change structure.

Before launching into a theoretical explanation it might be helpful to explain in colloquial language that what it amounts to is this: managers can specify roles, responsibilities and so forth. However, because of the way structure is enacted in practice, there may well be two organizations. That is, the one that exists as a figment of imagination or as a historical document that comprises the formal organization. The other is what actually happens in practice. Usually there is a fairly strong if imperfect correlation between the two – but not always. Besides, the two forms of organization can be pulled apart as actors interact with one another and as the environment changes.

In this chapter we are particularly concerned with how actors can manipulate structure for their own ends to achieve what sociologists call a change of script – in this case from a position of high subordination to one of domination.

Power and structure

What do we mean by structure? Control based perspectives of organization depict structure as a fixed and tangible entity as reflected, for example, in organization charts, job descriptions and codes of practice, instruction manuals and so forth. In this view structure resembles an architect's drawing. Although architects can specify where footpaths shall go in their plans, ultimately what defines a footpath is where people walk. Indeed, this is how medieval roads were created and recreated as travellers changed where they walked in order to avoid flooding and other perils.

Structure can be seen in much the same way, that is, as a pattern of continuous but dynamic relations between organized groups of actors (Giddens 1979). According to Giddens (1979, 1984), in performing their roles and relating to one another, actors draw upon rules (allocative and authoritative) and resources and in so doing end up changing those rules and resources. Moreover, whereas control based perspectives of organization view employees as intellectually limited, theory of structure depicts employees as knowledgeable and reflexive, that is, able to observe, act, understand their actions, and monitor the results. In other words, opportunities to commit malfeasance in organizations do not just exist 'out there' waiting to be discovered, but are to some extent created by organizational miscreants (discussed further in Sarason et al. 2006).

For instance, the introduction of screen based underwriting promised huge efficiency gains in the London insurance market. Yet brokers and underwriters shunned it because it upset the cultural ethos of the market:

> They [junior and middle level brokers and underwriters] like its [the market's] lack of structure, conviviality. The lack of surveillance … they chat among themselves as they call it 'gathering market intelligence' … They have an aura of mulling around the City doing big deals.
>
> (Barrett and Walsham 1999: 11)

Orlikowski (1996) observed that when technology was introduced enabling sales staff to record their interactions with customers directly into the computer system, most continued with paper and pen and then wrote up their records afterwards. Staff argued that hitting a keyboard disrupted conversations with customers and that a paper record was useful in the event of system failure. The real reason for resisting direct entry, however, was to enable staff to exercise editorial control over information that might reflect adversely upon them as once details were entered onto the system they could not be altered.

Viewing structure as *'recurrent social practices'* (Giddens 1979: 66, italics in original) implies that rules and practices coexist – in other words while actors create their structures (for example, by circumnavigating computer systems), they are to some extent created by them. Electronic markets may be resisted but they are here to stay even if the promised productivity gains are not fully realized. Recall, Hatch (1999) invokes the image of organizational structure as improvisational jazz. Hatch alludes to organizational actors as rather like jazz musicians influencing the tune to be played but also taking their cue from how it is *already* being played – that is, using structure to break out of structure:

> The improvisational practices of jazz constitute the conditions of its own structural transformation, even as the structures of jazz provide the starting point for improvisation ...
>
> Jazz musicians ... play their structures implicitly by explicitly *not* playing them and in doing so *play with* their structures in the dual senses of interacting with structure and altering it via improvisation.
>
> (Hatch 1999: 84, italics in original)

A control based bureaucratic perspective of organization centres assumes that the critical question actors pose is 'What structures shall we use?' The jazz metaphor highlights a subtly different possibility, namely, 'How shall we use our structures?'

How far can such improvisation go? According to Hatch (1999) jazz players do not take their tunes as given but play around them, interpreting them as loosely as possible, maximizing ambiguity. Yet as Hatch observes, there are risks and it does not always work. Sometimes players manage to 'find the groove' achieving harmony and rhythm with one another; other times they end up 'crashing' the tune. Crashes happen when players push the boundaries too far and discover that there are some things they cannot get away with.

The path to power

The licence application and setting up account 88888 doubtless taught Leeson that he could get away with quite a lot in Barings. Yet that was only the start. From a theoretical perspective, whereas notions of paradox and contradiction imply that organizational dynamics result in outcomes that are virtually a foregone conclusion, the theory of structure implies that nothing is inevitable. This is because the theory suggests that much depends upon how employees choose to interact with their structures and how their structures impact upon them over time. To mix metaphors, structural change can viewed as a kaleidoscope. Actors seldom start from a completely clean sheet but typically carve out their worlds from the available materials (Brown 1978; Hatch 1999). Patterns are formed and reformed in a way that is partly dependent on what has gone before and yet the new pattern is by no means predictable.

Early research into the impact of technology in organizations typically assumed a direct relationship between the type of technology employed and important variables like job satisfaction. In contrast more recent studies that have used theory of structure as a conceptual lens to study the impact of technological change suggest that earlier more 'broad brush' approaches may have missed subtle differences between apparently similar cases. For instance, Barley's (1986) detailed and nuanced study of the introduction of CCT scanners into hospitals discovered that while new technology can affect the balance of power between radiographers and technicians, these developments did not always translate into identical structural changes. Barley attributes these differential results to historical differences between the two organizations, suggesting that, 'Unintended and unanticipated consequences may nevertheless follow a contextual logic' (Barley 1986: 107). Likewise, Hatch (1999) notes that in improvisational jazz, it is the context that determines whether a 'wrong' note is or is not a mistake.

As we shall see later in this book, it can be argued quite plausibly that Barings' collapse was 'an accident waiting to happen' in view of the underdeveloped settlements function, particularly in Barings' overseas offices. Yet the Singapore office where Leeson worked was the least of Barings' worries because it was ably administered by Simon Jones, the local manager. Can theory of structure with its close-range focus upon patterns of interaction and changing social practices help to explain why the collapse happened where it was least likely?

In order to answer that question, it will be necessary to focus upon Leeson's role, what opportunities were available to him and how he exploited them. Whereas control based theories of organization typically view opportunity as something 'out there' waiting to be discovered, theory of structure implies that reflexive actors do not so much discover opportunities as create them. We saw in Chapters 4 and 5 that checks and balances intended to prevent opportunism can be used to facilitate it. Theory of structure takes a more fine-grained approach to analysis by focusing upon the interaction between the actor and potential sources of opportunity (Chiasson and Saunders 2005). This approach entails examining how employees influence opportunity and reflexively monitor the impact of their actions. For instance, the impact may be to reinforce, modify or create new opportunities according to their interpretations of and relations with structural context.

Scripts

Scripts provide the conceptual device for tracing the subtle shifts that contributed to the development of Leeson's power. Scripts focus attention upon *what* actually changes (e.g. Barley 1986; Barley and Tolbert 1997; Chiasson and Saunders 2005). For instance, Dell changed the script for desk top computers by selling exclusively through mail order. EasyJet changed the script in the passenger airline industry by offering cheap 'no frills' flights from neglected airports. NAXOS changed the script in the classical music industry by offering cheap recordings using relatively obscure artists and confining themselves to compositions on which copyright had expired. Access to web based knowledge means that patients know as much (and sometimes more) about their condition than the doctor who is treating them and can question the doctor's prescription accordingly. Consequently the script has changed from a relationship of authority to one that more closely resembles persuasion. By planting the grenade in the toilet, the 'guy' who has 'flipped out' achieves a small script change as the enemy 'within' becomes more lethal than the officially designated enemy 'without'.

To be more precise, scripts constitute the behavioural grammars that inform everyday action (Barley 1986). For example, a grammatical rule of commodities speculation is that no one actually takes delivery of the hogs, coffee beans, copper and so forth that they have contracted to buy or sell on a given date. Until, that was, an entrepreneur named Bunker Nelson Hunt surprised the market for silver in the early 1980s by insisting upon actual physical delivery of purchased quantities. Hunt's strategy was to corner supplies, thereby forcing the price of silver to rise astronomically and make a fortune. The market reacted to this attempted script change by instituting one of their own. Suddenly the market reversed the sacrosanct script of a free market as the Chicago Board of Trade decreed that all traders holding more than 600 contracts must reduce their positions immediately: 'You can't do that,' was Hunt's incredulous reaction. 'You wouldn't dare. You're the last bastion of free enterprise in the world' (Abolafia and Kilduff 1988: 177, citing Fay 1982: 138).

They could and they did. Moreover the Chicago Board continued to make changes in the script to control what it regarded as an artificial (illegitimate) attempt to inflate the price of silver at the expense of others. 'Hunt found himself confronted by an organization with the power to redefine the rules of transaction and the temerity to violate the sacrosanct principles of a free market' (Abolafia and Kilduff 1988: 177).

Not all script changes in complex organizations are as dramatic. Although control based theories of organization assume stability as the normal state of affairs whereas theory of structure presupposes organizations exist in a constant state of flux and transformation, profound change need not entail violent upheaval:

> Because of the magnitude of some changes in organizations, we are inclined to look for comparably dramatic explanations for change, but the search for drama may often be a mistake ... Change takes place because most of the time people in an organization do more or less what they are supposed to do; that is they are intelligently attentive to their environments and their jobs.
>
> (March 1981: 546; see also Feldman 2000; Mintzberg 1993;
> Orlikowski 1996: 65)

The idea that most people in organizations attempt to follow the script most of the time does not mean that scripts change by a process of mutation. Barley (1986) suggests that something has to happen to provide a trigger or occasion for change, such as the introduction of new technology or methods and practices. The question then becomes in what ways might these triggers result in change? How do resourceful (reflexive) actors utilize rules and resources to obtain their ends and how do they deal with constraints? For instance, although the so-called five-eights account provided cover for Leeson's illicit trading, his use of the account would have been discovered if he had been supervised as Barings clearly intended. What happened to trigger this script change?

Barley (1986) further suggests that script change will be a complex multilayered process that twists and turns over time. That said, Chiasson and Saunders (2005, citing Giddens 1984) suggest that the development of power is likely to follow a three stage process of signification, legitimation and domination. Signification refers to framing, articulating and interpreting possibilities. Signification imparts meaning in social interactions. According to Chiasson and Saunders (2005), signification is particularly important during the discovery of opportunities. It can be argued that demand for a product or service does not just exist objectively ('out there') but becomes real as entrepreneurs interact with potential customers and create it. For example, government sponsored health promotion campaigns in the UK urging people to eat five pieces of fruit a day have prompted some entrepreneurially minded retailers to offer customers prepackaged trays containing five small pieces of fruit. The impetus may have come from the government but the trick in converting the campaign into a commercial opportunity was packaging the fruit in a manner that made it affordable and easy to carry.

Legitimation structures provide evaluation criteria (values) for dispensing rewards and sanctions. Chiasson and Saunders (2005) predict that legitimation is most important during the early development phase via the application of protocols and the development of relationships by knowledgeable reflexive actors. The sustained safety record of low cost airline companies has helped to build legitimacy among travellers. Dell's script change was legitimized as customers began to trust mail order, eventually propelling Dell to a position of being able to contest the domination of other leading manufacturers such as HP/Compac. The introduction of so-called 'top up' fees in universities promises a script change if students assume consumer power. Conversely Hunt failed to achieve domination because his strategy was declared illegitimate.

Domination structures are transformative relationships that facilitate goal attainment through acquiring control over material and human resources. For example, Chiasson and Saunders (2005) note that in the 1600s private lighthouse keepers solved the problem of non-payers by persuading the government to institute a toll at ports. In other words, lighthouse keepers achieved domination by creating institutions that would enable them to generate a profit. A more modern example of a domination structure might be Microsoft's pervasive Windows Operating System. The so-called 'Army Rumour Web Site' (ARS but more colloquially known as ARSE) is an example of a new structure that is attempting to challenge an old domination structure as the website exists to countermand the official view of the British Army. It can be seen as part of a wider script change within the armed forces where traditional command and control structures are being challenged in ways that would have been unthinkable in another era.

8   From order filler to star trader

I was totally out of control.

(Leeson 1997: 141)

'A structure that will prove disastrous ... '

Leeson's secondment to Singapore was confirmed by a fax to James Bax, the area manager. The fax said that Leeson would 'head up our Simex operation and also act as floor manager ... he will report to Simon Jones and Gordon Bowser' (Board of Banking Supervision 1995: 31). Bax was not pleased. He wanted Leeson to be responsible to Jones alone: 'Once again we are in danger of setting up a structure which will subsequently prove disastrous ... In my view it is critical that we should keep clear reporting lines', he wrote (Board of Banking Supervision 1995: 31).

It is unclear what Bax meant by 'once again' but he may well have been alluding to the perilous state of settlements in Barings Securities where there had been more emphasis upon building the business than developing the detailed administrative infrastructure needed to support expansion. The New York office had unsettled trades dating back two years and the authorities were threatening to revoke Barings' licence. In late 1992 a trader in the Hong Kong office was discovered selling options without authority in collusion with the back office, prompting a local manager to write to Andrew Baylis, Barings' deputy chairman:

> The settlements area is struggling ... we will inevitably incur large trading errors if we do not make this a top priority area ... I have found out that we never properly collected hundreds of millions of Yen in margin money to begin with [and] there are many other 'bigger' 'potentially HUGE' problems to be sorted ...
>
> Andrew, you know how much money we lost in interest income last year ... Millions of pounds. Do you know we have a temp handling all our margin money? Do you know that the margin regularly represents multiples of net worth of the entire company?
>
> (Ministry for Finance, Singapore 1995: 65)

In contrast the Singapore office seemed fairly efficient, thanks to the efforts of Simon Jones, the local manager. Jones, however, was perceived in London as parochial and uncooperative. Bax's protest was ignored because the joint supervision arrangement was a device to limit Jones' authority.

As it turned out Gordon Bowser, Risk Manager for Barings Securities (then based in London), was unable to exercise effective supervision over Leeson because he was too far away. Jones was separated from Leeson by ten floors of office block. He responded to requests for advice from Leeson but was never really proactive in controlling him.

Besides, close supervision seemed superfluous because Leeson was a model employee. Barings aimed to build a sales team in Singapore. The installation of an English speaking manager was an important part of implementing that strategy. Thanks to Leeson communications between Osaka and Singapore improved dramatically and before long a small but profitable business was underway between the two offices (Ministry for Finance, Singapore 1995: 10).

Suspense accounts

Leeson's main contact in Japan was Mike Killian, Head of Futures and Options Sales. Killian would telephone orders to Leeson, who would then transmit them by hand signals to traders stationed on the floor of SIMEX. Recall, Leeson made a lot of mistakes learning how to execute trades, which he then hid in the five-eights account. At this juncture it is necessary to explain the role of error accounts in more detail. By long established practice in the securities industry, errors are settled internally. There is no question of trying to renegotiate the price with the client. The options for dealing with failed trades include reallocating the contracts to another order, selling them to another customer or placing them somehow – the aim being to minimize the loss. One stratagem might be to telephone other traders who might also be trying to place errors. 'Strictly speaking we weren't allowed to deal after SIMEX closed, but everybody called around trying to balance their books in the late afternoon' (Leeson 1997: 62). Alternatively traders would hang on to contracts for a few days hoping for favourable market movement. Strictly speaking this was propriety trading but at such low levels the exposure to risk was negligible. Indeed Leeson had discretion about when to close off positions so long as limits were observed and no positions were left open overnight. The overnight restriction was in place because so much could change in the intervening hours (Ministry for Finance, Singapore 1995: 18). Leeson would circumnavigate that rule by getting colleagues in Japan to hold contracts overnight. They did it as a favour believing that Leeson was acting for a customer.

Error accounts are basically suspense accounts. Suspense accounts have other uses. Fund managers sometimes buy blocks of contracts. At busy times brokers might place combined orders. Blocks and combined orders are initially held in a suspense account pending reallocation of specific contracts to individual customers. Suspense accounts might also be used as 'shock absorbers' for losses. Sometimes it would prove impossible to obtain a price promised to a customer.

For example, a market might move even as a trade was being executed. Again, Barings would honour its promise and stand the resultant loss.

Brokers might also discount prices in order to attract business. Since SIMEX rules did not encourage such practices, the sale would be recorded in an account showing the lower price and the corresponding loss would be booked to a suspense account. Normally this would be done by an assistant sitting in a booth adjacent to the trading pit recording ongoing adjustments. Such practices were routine in Barings and traders might operate as many as twenty-five suspense accounts.

'Unthinkable in any other bank ...'

A scam Leeson discovered early on involved accepting client orders at a given price, then dealing upon the cheapest exchange (Osaka or SIMEX) and Barings would pocket the difference (Ministry for Finance, Singapore 1995: 19). More importantly, Leeson's colleagues in Japan were impressed with his knack of beating market rates when executing trades and started charging clients extra for his services. Before long (it is not clear exactly when) Leeson's colleagues stopped specifying prices, trusting him to use his discretion.

While Leeson could see prices in Osaka on the computer screen, as SIMEX was open outcry, Leeson's colleagues in Japan had to rely on him for information on prices. This meant they had no idea what price Leeson actually obtained when executing trades. In fact Leeson was underpricing business, hiding the resultant losses in the five-eights account and hoping to trade out of it later. Moreover, since Leeson was also responsible for settling trades, he could (and did) adjust prices between accounts and send 'doctored' lists of transactions to colleagues in Japan. In July 1992 Leeson lost about £40,000 of Barings' money in this way. By the end of August that amount had reached £320,000 – enough to earn Leeson the sack yet only a miniscule fraction of what was to come (Ministry for Finance, Singapore 1995: 23).

In October 1992 a local trader made a mistake that threatened to cost Barings £150,000. This was too large a sum to conceal in the five-eights account indefinitely. Leeson sat down to map out the problem on a sheet of paper. He realized that while he could probably bluff London into sending money, saying it was to cover a client position, that would postpone the problem only until the month end. A longer term solution was required:

> I needed dollars and I needed yen, and I needed them totally at my discretion ... As I scribbled around the boxes, it dawned on me that if I sold options, I would actually receive a premium ... – this would be in yen, and I would be able to use it to balance the deficit in the 88888 account.
>
> (Leeson 1997: 80)

Leeson's plan to sell options would work only if London agreed to pay collateral known as margin. Since Leeson had no authority to sell options, he could not request payment openly. Instead, he pretended that he was acting for a customer from whom Barings would subsequently recoup payment:

> This would be unthinkable in any other bank ... but my lines of communication with London were so vague that nobody knew who I reported to, and they tended to let me get on with the job.
>
> (Leeson 1997: 82)

But who was the customer? No one knew for certain but that did not stop the funds from flowing out of London. When Leeson first took up the appointment in Singapore, Gordon Bowser wrote to Jones, Bax and Leeson stressing the need for daily reconciliation of margin funds to customer positions (Ministry for Finance, Singapore 1995: 25). Had that task been performed as directed, the deception would have been revealed. Bowser assumed that his advice was being adhered to. In fact, it was ignored and there was no reconciliation.

Moreover, Barings' controls had been developed for agency rather than propriety business. Consequently staffing levels could not cope with the more complex back office work where a mix of trades was involved. Leeson used this weakness to 'fiddle' accounts so that SIMEX called for less margin than required under the rules, while calls were manipulated so that London remitted more funding than was required – the surplus being used to fund the five-eights account (Ministry for Finance, Singapore 1995: 25).

A naked gamble

Although trading options is a very risky business, it can be profitable if done properly. Leeson's approach involved naked gambling. There is a distinction between risk-taking and gambling. Gambling refers to probabilities of losses that are unacceptably high and gains that are unacceptably low (e.g. Yates and Stone 1992). Professional traders take risks but they use sophisticated mathematical models to calculate the premium needed to offset the risk. Lacking the necessary mathematical knowledge to calculate the requisite premium, Leeson sold too cheaply and therefore lost money. Even more seriously, whereas professional traders limit their exposure by matching a contract to buy with an equal and opposite contract to sell and vice versa, since Leeson needed to maximize the amount of premium obtained, he could not afford the luxury of matched positions. When his options lost money, he simply sold more. By the end of 1992 Leeson had lost about £2 million in failed options trading.

'He is a star!'

Since the premium obtained from those illicit sales was booked as pure profit, Leeson appeared successful. Barings' annual report for 1993 made particularly pleasant reading for Leeson. In 1993 Barings Securities' total profits were £100 million – £35 million from Asia, including £10 million attributable to Leeson's trading. Leeson realized he was becoming an important contributor to the bonus pool.

That 'fact' would become increasingly apparent in London during the first half of 1994. The precise dates about who learned what and when they learned it are unclear. Certainly as late as December 1993, Peter Norris, Barings' chief executive, still believed that Leeson's role merely involved executing agency and propriety trades (Ministry for Finance, Singapore 1995: 10). In early 1994 Ron Baker, Head of Financial Products Group, and Mary Waltz, Global Head of Equity Financial Products, visited Japan and discovered that Leeson was trading in his own right and earning profits from arbitrage – profits that had eluded Leeson's colleagues in Japan when they attempted it.

Baker apparently swallowed Leeson's story about being ideally positioned to anticipate the emergence of price differentials. Baker (and Waltz's) limited experience of options trading facilitated deception: 'He seemed to me to be a blue eyed boy,' said Baker (Secretary of State versus Baker np).

Excited by the possibilities, Baker quietly resolved to become Leeson's line manager so that Leeson's profits would become part of the Financial Product Group's accounts (Ministry for Finance, Singapore 1995: 36). Shortly after the visit Baker sent two undated memoranda to Peter Norris. The first comprised an explanation of Leeson's trading where Baker referred to Leeson and his colleagues in Japan as:

> natural traders whose desire to absorb and manage risk is now balancing more effectively the pure arbitrage mentality of Gueler and Brindle ... In short they are emerging as an exciting team who will continue to develop and who should be encouraged.
>
> (Secretary of State versus Baker np)

The second memorandum concerned bonus payments for 1993. Referring to Leeson as someone Norris should 'care about ... He is a star!' (Secretary of State versus Baker np), Baker recommended Leeson for a bonus of £320,000. Baker's enthusiasm concealed fear:

> Not only did they [i.e. Mr Gueler and other propriety traders at BSJ] tell me that their bonuses were critical, and that they would leave if they did not get them, they also made it very, very clear that Nick was part of their world in terms of how much money he generated ... and [that] it was extremely important that Nick got looked after as well, because if Nick did not get looked after, then he would go as well.
>
> (Secretary of State versus Baker np)

Baker's judgement appeared to be swiftly vindicated. For the first seven months of 1994 Leeson earned £25 million out of the Financial Product Group's total of £50 million.

Peter Norris was impressed but concerned. Where *exactly* were these profits coming from? Norris may have been influenced by a memorandum from Waltz about trading in the Far East stating that despite 'the many safety nets at our finger tips ... there is currently no limit at all on the size of things we do, or on the net position what we may take (however safety netted) as we are trading' (Secretary of State versus Baker np)

Norris requested a breakdown of trades. Waltz, apparently fearing that Norris intended to divert profits away from the Financial Products Group, seems not to have complied (Secretary of State versus Baker np).

In April 1994 Ron Baker reported to the Risk Committee (subsequently ALCO, note copied to the Management Committee, MANCO) that Fernando Gueler's team had started arbitraging Japanese Government Bonds between SIMEX and Tokyo and that formal risk proposals would be put before the committee in May. In fact, limits were not imposed until 16 June 1994. Even then Baker never checked whether those limits were being observed despite emerging evidence that strongly suggested not. For instance, in May 1994 Baker commissioned an analysis of levels of liquidity in and around Singapore. It is unclear what Baker subsequently did with the data but it would have shown him that the market was increasing in size, becoming more liquid and therefore offering *less* opportunity for price anomaly arbitrage. Yet Baker never questioned Leeson about it.

Leeson managed to clear his losses during 1993. His status as a 'star trader' had become an addiction, however, and one that could be fed only by selling options (Leeson 1997). That addiction included trading for a customer named Philippe Bonnefoy, who traded thousands of contracts. It was good business but Bonnefoy drove a hard bargain on price. Leeson responded by 'legging it', that is, promising a price the trader cannot at present meet, effectively taking a propriety position against yourself. Traders typically have authority to take 100 propriety contracts. Thanks to Bonnefoy, Leeson soon found himself sitting on almost 2000.

'Leeson has too much power and influence'

In July 1992 Barings noticed that it appeared to have paid out about £10 million more in margin calls to Singapore than it had collected from customers. Since clients are required to pay margin promptly the problem should not exist, but Group Treasury had never asked Leeson why long term funding was required. A subsequent investigation proved inconclusive and the discrepancy was attributed to time lags between London and Singapore. By early 1994, however, the unreconciled amount was nearing £100 million. Something must be done.

Before, Leeson always had time to think about how to conceal his losses because no one would ever require an immediate account. In early 1994 that situation was about to change as Barings directed an internal auditor named Ash Lewis to investigate Leeson's unusual profits and the reconciliation problem. In fact, the auditor's brief listed several concerns:

1   Leeson might be breaking local rules and 'has too much power and influence' (Board of Banking Supervision 1995: 143; concern identified by Gordon Bowser).

2   'Leeson has too dominant a role looking after both trading ... and settlements aspects of the business; there is no deputy to challenge him. The amounts of money involved are vast' (Board of Banking Supervision 1995: 143; concern identified by Tony Hawes, Treasurer of Barings Investment Bank).

3   'The level of margin calls ... without knowing precisely on who's [*sic*] behalf the cash is being paid ... Tony would at least like to know how much of the payment is for house positions and how much is for customers' (Board of Banking Supervision 1995: 143; concern identified by Tony Hawes).

Ash Lewis had a reputation for perspicacity and tenacity and Leeson felt as if he were a skeleton being X-rayed (Leeson 1997). Fortunately for Leeson and unfortunately for Barings, Lewis was recalled to London before she could discover anything incriminating. Her place was taken by James Baker and Ian Manson. They spent a month in Singapore repeatedly interviewing Leeson and poring over his records.

It was a nerve-wracking experience for Leeson because the evidence of mal feasance was everywhere. Surely the auditors would ask to see a printout of account 88888? Additionally or alternatively they might request a summary of positions reported to SIMEX, which would also reveal the existence of the five-eights account and losses contained therein. Surely they would request sight of a balance sheet and notice that, despite the apparent match between assets and liabilities on paper, half the money remitted from London to margin calls had gone to fund losses hidden in account 88888? Leeson had no authority to remove money from bank accounts but he could transfer monies between accounts – and shuffle he did. If the auditors looked closely at the Citibank records, they must see that far from holding £50 million as suggested in Leeson's summary position, the account was actually empty. 'Their eyebrows would hit the roof just as far as their jaws hit the ground' (Leeson 1997: 118).

Leeson need not have worried. In accounting parlance, 'no detailed testing of records was undertaken' and consequently the auditors saw nothing wrong. 'They completely missed what was staring me in the face every time I went back to my desk,' said Leeson (1996: 121).

The auditors' report was published in October 1994. It was largely reassuring. Leeson's profits were described as resulting from 'strong agency flows, unique execution capacity and a communications edge' (Board of Banking Supervision 1995: 124) and the whole operation was pronounced generally sound. The report concludes: 'Nothing we have reviewed suggests that BFS is obtaining an unfair advantage by breaking SIMEX rules nor taking positions in excess of limits' (Board of Banking Supervision 1995: 126).

There was just one snag, however. 'My only real source of enquiries with respect to the profitability review and much of the audit review was discussions with Nick Leeson', said James Baker (Board of Banking Supervision 1995: 144). James Baker is a chartered accountant but he struggled to understand Leeson's trading. One reason why his recommendations for detailed reconciliation were deleted from the draft report was that Baker was baffled by Leeson's explanation as to why the task was impossible. Transaction testing was also omitted from the audit because some of Leeson's documents were incomprehensible (Ministry for Finance, Singapore 1995: 36–38). Leeson's account of how he made his profits was equally obscure:

> Leeson spoke rapidly about crossing a leg here and giving a tick here. Baker [the auditor] would ask him to go over it again, struggling to grasp enough to write an explanation in plain English. He unwittingly became Leeson's ghost-writer in a work of fiction.
>
> (Gapper and Denton 1996: 255)

'A significant general risk ...'

Not all of the audit report was fiction. The auditors noted that it was theoretically possible for non-existent trades to be booked and extra margin called as there was no check to ensure that amounts requested by Leeson and the margin calls actually issued by SIMEX matched. In an initial draft the auditors recommended a daily reconciliation of funding requirements to minimize the risk. James Baker said, 'The main point for me was to ensure that margin was not being siphoned off by Singapore ... I thought that reconciliation would ... stop any danger' (Board of Banking Supervision 1995: 146).

Indeed it would. After flattering the auditors, 'You've really got this operation taped,' Leeson said, 'The only thing is that the daily reconciliation is going to be very difficult to do, because of the timing differences' (Leeson 1997: 121). James Baker replied that daily reconciliation was unnecessary: it could be done monthly by a clerk and would take about two days. James Baker was supported by Geoff Broadhurst, Group Finance Director of Barings Investment Bank, who was visiting Singapore when the audit report was being drafted. Relations between Simon Jones and Broadhurst were bad, however. The two men were barely on speaking terms. Jones supported Leeson and eventually the suggestion was dropped.

The auditors also recommended that Leeson's accounts be made subject to regular and frequent scrutiny by an independent risk and compliance officer – namely Gordon Bowser. This was more dangerous to Leeson than regular reconciliation. If the latter had been implemented, the reconciliation clerk would at least have been supervised by Leeson. Bowser was senior to Leeson; he would be watching him directly and was hardly amenable to manipulation. Again Jones (fearing a Trojan horse) came to Leeson's rescue, arguing that there was insufficient work for a full-time appointment. Eventually after some desultory discussions, an appointment on the lines suggested by Jones was made with effect from 1 March 1995 – allowing time for the person appointed to serve notice. By then, however, Barings no longer existed.

By mid-1994 business had grown in Singapore so much that the internal auditors decided that Leeson should now relinquish control of settlement.

Unsurprisingly Leeson had other ideas. In August 1994 Ron Baker visited Singapore again and had lunch with James Bax. According to Bax, Leeson was 'touchy' about the possibly of losing the general manager role, of which he was apparently very proud. Bax told Baker:

> Leeson has been a back office guy all his life and he does not know whether this trading will last forever and he is clearly loathe to burn his bridges with one career before he is totally certain of another career.
>
> (Secretary of State versus Baker np)

Again, James Baker was forced to retract. The executive summary of the audit report noted that:

> While the individual controls over BFS's system and operations are satisfactory, there is a significant general risk that controls could be overridden by the general manager.
>
> (Board of Banking Supervision 1995: 146)

This 'significant general risk' was resolved by a compromise:

> In normal circumstances it would not be desirable for one individual to combine the roles of dealing with those of settlements and accounting manager. Given the lack of experienced and senior staff in the back office, we recognise that the General Manager must continue to take an active role in the detailed operations of the front and back office.
>
> (Board of Banking Supervision 1995: 147)

Compromise notwithstanding, the audit report made recommendations that might have saved Barings if they had been implemented in a timely and effective manner. Those recommendations included reorganizing the back office and removing Leeson's sole responsibility for supervising staff, his journal passing off powers and his responsibility for reviewing and signing off reconciliations. If those recommendations had been implemented, the various tasks would have been transferred to the accounts department in Singapore, where they would have been beyond Leeson's control.

Indeed, when the audit report was published, Leeson and Jones immediately announced that, 'With immediate effect, the General Manager will cease to perform the functions itemised' (Board of Banking Supervision 1995: 149). Nothing happened. No one from London checked to see that Jones had implemented the recommendations. Recall that the Head of Compliance did not read the report. Neither did Ron Baker (Secretary of State versus Baker np). Andrew Tuckey, Barings' deputy chairman, did not receive a copy. Nor did he request one (Secretary of State versus Tuckey np).

Tony Hawes learned that the internal auditors had left the reconciliation problem untouched. James Baker said, 'I think from the evidence of my brief conversation,

I concluded that certainly in a short time it was *difficult to give even a split between house and client* and thus I had to throw it back into Treasury's court' (Board of Banking Supervision 1995: 148, italics added). Accordingly the auditors recommended that Treasury should conduct its own review, 'over the coming year' (Board of Banking Supervision 1995: 148).

It was an unlooked for task but apparently not urgent. Having read the report, Hawes was relieved to learn that no undue risks were being run in Singapore. Hawes subsequently said that as the report made 'no mention at all of what I saw as the excess margin there ... It moved my anxiety down a couple of notches' (Board of Banking Supervision 1995: 150).

'An important grey area ...'

Another paragraph deleted from the draft audit report referred to 'an important grey area' (Board of Banking Supervision 1995: 146), namely the practice of running house positions in excess of intra-day limits and hedging those positions by a client order. It is unclear why or how this comment came to be deleted. Significantly it implied the possibility of insider trading and suggested that Leeson was habitually trading beyond his intra-day limits.

Those limits were 200 Nikkei futures, 100 Japanese Government Bonds and 500 Euroyen. When the auditors left Singapore, Leeson had over 20,000 contracts. To set that figure in perspective, before Leeson arrived in Singapore, SIMEX traded 5000 contracts a day. By the end of 1994 trades were approaching 20,000 contracts. Leeson accounted for approximately 20 per cent of the total, prompting SIMEX to name him 'trader of the year'.

Yet neither Waltz nor Baker questioned Leeson about whether he was breaking his limits (Secretary of State versus Baker np). Nor did Waltz question Leeson's assurance that all his positions were matched. Leeson said:

> If she'd stopped to think about it she'd have known I couldn't have sold that number on SIMEX to buy back on Osaka but she never said anything to me and had clearly not told Ron Baker that I was totally out of control.
>
> (Leeson 1997: 141)

Apparently no one else thought about it either. The minutes of the Risk Committee for 19 October 1994 record that 'RB [Ron Baker] confirmed that there has been no indication of any breach in NL's [Leeson's] intra-day limit' (Secretary of State versus Baker np). Yet this was the week that reported revenues for Japanese Government Bond arbitrage alone were £3.638 million. How could Leeson have generated revenues of this magnitude without breaking his intra-day limits of 500 contracts? The minutes of the Risk Committee do not record that anyone even posed the question, far less demanded an answer.

According to Leeson, Baker was more interested in empire building by replicating his alleged arbitrage business in Tokyo and Hong Kong. Leeson encouraged the dream, engaging Baker in dialogue about 'using trading books in a way that supplements customer requirements and increases the information flow on both sides' and other such 'mumbo jumbo'. Leeson said:

> Hiding losses from these people was so easy. They were always too busy and too self-important ... They could not make the time to work through a sheet of numbers and spot that it didn't add up.
>
> (Leeson 1997: 192)

9 Analysis of Leeson's early days

Before Leeson arrived, Singapore was a backwater. Leeson's installation as office manager triggers a change of script: Singapore becomes more important as Leeson becomes the focal point for the development of trade. Recall that signification, the process of framing, articulating and interpreting possibilities, is likely to be most important early on in the discovery and creation of opportunities. Leeson both discovers and creates opportunities to create a good impression by establishing himself in various ways as a credible manager. He does this by zealous attention to the needs of his employer and in particular his colleagues in Japan.

The most important opportunity is the hairline crack that opens up as the dual supervision arrangement proves unworkable – as Bax predicted. The proposed template envisaging matrix management is fairly unambiguous. The trouble is that it is not taken seriously by the actors involved. The recurrent social practice (structure) that develops sees Leeson as largely self-supervising.

Recall, Hatch (1999) suggests that players use structure in order to escape from structure by taking their cue from the tune that is already being played. Leeson starts small, taking his cue from traders' existing creative use of suspense accounts. Having recognized the possibilities inherent in account 888888 being disconnected from reporting systems, Leeson uses the account to hide more substantial errors. Mis-pricing business was an extension of the practice of 'legging it'. Colleagues cooperate with small rule infringements such as holding contracts overnight and trading practices that are inconsistent with SIMEX's rules. The small propriety trading that takes place on a small scale in order to avoid taking losses provides the cue for subsequent options trading.

Technology helps as the opaque structure of SIMEX means that Leeson's colleagues in Japan cannot obtain independent verification of prices. Ultimately Leeson gets away with it, however, because he is unsupervised. This is the 'contextual logic' (Barley 1986) that renders malfeasance on a large scale much more probable than it would otherwise be.

Legitimation

Recall that legitimation refers to gaining social acceptance. Leeson's responsiveness to his colleagues' needs provides the first plank in establishing his legitimacy.

His apparent ability to beat market rates added to it. The most important evidence of Leeson's growing legitimacy is reflected in colleagues' decision to stop specifying prices. Recall, March (1981) suggests that change occurs in organizations because most people stick fairly closely to the script most of the time. This slight but important shift in recurrent social practices happens because specifying prices has become redundant as (apparently) Leeson invariably beats market rates, so the structure gets used in a different way as his colleagues in Japan allow him maximum headway. They do it because they trust him. Trust is a heuristic: it lowers the transaction costs of doing business because it obviates the need for people to check up on one another.

This oblique shift has another important consequence because it transports Leeson from being a mere order filler to de facto trader. Leeson subsequently uses structure to escape from structure as his newfound status enables him to start selling options without authority. Leeson's decision to sell options is the most important trigger in the present study because the reported revenues from this activity put him firmly on the road to domination. It is a deliberate and carefully calculated decision as Leeson weighs up the possibilities in a reflexive fashion, deciding that he needed yen and mapping out the possibilities.

Leeson gets away with it because his roles are completely unsegregated. It happens because of the way in which Leeson's role has evolved, that is from office manager into trading. The aforementioned hairline crack becomes like the San Andreas fault line as Leeson is simultaneously poacher and gamekeeper. During 1993 Leeson's profits grow but he is not immediately visible because his activities are subsumed under those of Barings' operations in Japan. By the time Ron Baker and Peter Norris learn that Leeson is actually trading, he is already well established.

Signification, legitimation and domination may overlap. The annual report for 1993 is a mark of signification. It imparts meaning as it identifies Leeson as an important profit centre. Leeson's contribution is subsequently legitimized by the payment of a substantial bonus as Ron Baker names him a 'star'. Legitimation is shading into domination however, as Leeson successfully pressurizes Baker to pay him more as he is no longer a mere order filler.

Waltz unsuccessfully tries to challenge Leeson's freedom to conduct limitless arbitrage. Norris does not pursue the issue and besides Leeson is veering out of control. Another sign of domination is that Leeson starts trading in Japanese Government Bonds (JGB) without authority. Paradoxically, by setting limits on Leeson's JGB trading, Baker effectively legitimizes it. Little ambiguity surrounds those limits but Leeson ignores them – another sign of growing domination.

Since in any case Baker never checked to ensure that those limits were being observed, what purpose do they serve? It was suggested in Chapter 3 that organizations sometimes manipulate symbols and symbolic activity to create an air of respectability. Imposing limits creates the impression of responsible management and suggests that things are under control. Limit setting may also have been a political ploy aimed at paving the way for identifying Leeson's trading with Baker's Financial Products Group and for Leeson's profits to be booked to Baker's group accordingly.

Towards domination

Leeson's growing domination is also reflected in the auditor's brief where he is described as having too much power. The internal audit might have triggered a reversion of the script as it was a clear opportunity to expose malfeasance well before extremely serious damage occurred. The opportunity was lost because the auditors were forced to dilute or delete their most dangerous recommendations. Leeson's domination is by no means complete, however. He depended for his survival on support from powerful actors interested in seeing off the auditors for their own reasons. Baker supports Leeson because he wants to keep his star trader happy. Bax and Jones support Leeson because they perceive that it is in their interests to minimize London's involvement in the business of Barings Securities Singapore.

In fact, the internal audit report actually helps Leeson by unwittingly legitimizing his unauthorized trading. The auditors say that they have seen nothing to suggest that Barings is taking unfair advantage of knowledge of customer positions, thereby legitimizing the practice of 'front running' (insider trading). The auditors acknowledge a 'significant general risk' that controls could be overridden by the general manager, but the language is far from alarmist. Moreover the auditors leave the reconciliation problem untouched. Few organizations achieve perfect reconciliation. In this case, however, £100 million is unaccounted for. Since the auditors do not raise the alarm, other actors including Tony Hawes feel justified in taking their time to deal with the issues. All in all, the effect of the audit report on those who bothered to read it is to sound a 'false all clear'.

If Bax and Jones had followed through their announcement that Leeson would cease to perform certain back office functions, malfeasance might have been exposed. In fact they do nothing and no one from London checks up on them. If actions speak louder than words (e.g. Salancik and Pfeffer 1977), then the fact that key actors did not even read the internal audit report speaks volumes about the ordering of priorities within Barings.

Beyond greed

The lay reader might say that the preceding analysis dissolves into one word: 'greed'. It is it is more than that, however. Important recommendations were actually deleted from the audit report partly because the auditors were baffled by Leeson's accounts. Mary Waltz too accepted a nonsensical explanation about how he earned his profits almost without question. Baker clearly did not understand Leeson's trading either. Yet everyone pretended that they were *au fait* with Leeson's alleged business.

Such behaviour is consistent with social sciences theories of self-enhancement that suggest suboptimal decisions may get made because we are reluctant to appear foolish to ourselves and to significant others (summarized in Pfeffer and Fong 2005; see also Staw 1981, 1997; Staw and Ross 1987; Teger 1980). We shall return to this theme later in this book. Here we need only note that key actors were out of their depth. Their reluctance to admit it to one another facilitated Leeson's domination.

10 Decision error

He who rides a tiger can never dismount.

(Chinese proverb)

We come now to the last few weeks of the bank's existence, when the danger signs were clearly visible. The nature of those warning signs is recounted in the next chapter. Here it is sufficient to note that Barings either missed them altogether or saw them but failed to act in an effective and timely manner.

The purpose of this chapter is to outline theories of decision error and in particular to suggest why individuals and organizations are sometimes unable to see the wood for the trees, and why although they may see something amiss they may be unwilling or unable to take corrective action thus allowing problems to escalate. Although the various theories are presented individually, it should be borne in mind that research by social scientists suggests that in reality the reasons for escalation in organizations are likely to be complex and multifaceted (e.g. Drummond 1994, 1996; Ross and Staw 1986, 1993).

Psychological and social influences

Economic theory suggests that decision-making is guided by rationality. Economic theory thus portrays decision-makers approaching problems objectively and analytically, aiming to maximize utility. Research by social scientists suggests that in reality, rationality is not so much a guide as an achievement, a symbolic product where decision-makers gather and analyse information to make decision seem rational when in fact they are typically influenced with myriad non-rational influences.

Ego-defensiveness is a key non-rational influence (e.g. Brockner 1992). In a nutshell, as the proverb 'he who rides a tiger' suggests, once we become committed to a course of action we tend to become personally identified with it and may be held responsible for its subsequent success or failure. Quite simply most people prefer to be proved right than wrong – particularly if the decision-maker's career is at stake (see especially Fox and Staw 1979; Staw 1976). Persistence with a questionable course of action may enable the decision-maker to postpone the painful experience of having to acknowledge failure. It is also a way of signalling that the initial course of action was justified even though to an objective bystander feedback might indicate otherwise.

Agency may give added impetus to unwarranted persistence. To be more precise, failure creates a conflict of interests that employees as agents have to resolve. Agency refers to a contract in which the principal delegates authority to another person to perform on their behalf. The agent thus faces a conflict between acting in the best interests of the principal or in their own rational self-interest, that is, 'Thinking and acting in a manner that is expected to lead to an optimal or maximum result for the person on the basis of a consideration of the person's values and risk preferences' (Meglino and Korsgaard 2004). Agency theory posits that agents may continue with a course of action that is detrimental to the organization rather than risk sending a probabilistic signal that a decision was wrong.

Besides, decision-makers are typically slow to recognize reality. This is because they are thought to cognitively distort information to fit their preconceived views. In other words, as human beings we possess an innate tendency to hear what we want to hear while downplaying or even ignoring potentially ominous information. Since this tends to happen unconsciously decision-makers may thus become genuinely convinced that 'all's well' when the opposite is true (e.g. Staw and Ross 1987). For example, would-be litigants may receive identical information about a case and yet come to different conclusions about the likely outcome depending on whether they are plaintiffs or defendants.

The psychology of loss

Prospect theory offers a different but possibly complementary explanation for decision error. Recall that the theory predicts that escalation results from the manner in which choices are framed – positive or negative. Negative framing refers to a choice between losses. That is, when decision-makers must choose between accepting a definite loss here and now, or possibly avoiding that loss but at the risk of subsequently incurring a much greater one, they are likely to become risk seeking and take a bigger risk than an objective analysis of the situation warrants. That is, rather than accept a small loss, they typically risk a much greater one (Kahneman and Tversky 1982; see also Bazerman 2005; Whyte 1986, 1991b).

Prospect theory was developed to explain decisions involving clear-cut choices with defined mathematical consequences. Yet it may be relevant to domains where the issues are less precise. For example, would-be litigants may persist with a risky case rather than incur a defined loss for a relatively small sum in costs but at the risk of subsequently incurring huge liability if they lose. Whyte (1991a, 1991b) has argued that the decision to launch the ill-fated rocket *Challenger* was taken despite engineers' reservations about the reliability of the rocket seals because NASA was anxious not to lose political support for the programme. In the mid-1980s Coca-Cola changed the formula for Coke even though Coke was the world's largest selling soft drink. The decision was taken because Coke's market share had been declining. 'You can extrapolate that out and end up with zilch,' said Roberto Goizueta, Coke's president and chief operating officer (Whyte, citing Caminiti 1987: 48).

In their efforts to avoid loss, the decision-makers made a calamitous mistake that was reversed after three months. If the authorities had insisted upon a localized cull when BSE (bovine spongiform encephalopathy) first appeared in cattle, they might have prevented the subsequent epidemic. It was the reluctance to slaughter a few hundred animals that eventually led to the loss of thousands. In the late 1990s Shell responded to impending decline by quietly reworking the method for calculating reserves. The company then ignored internal warnings that it was over-stating its reserves of oil and gas for years because Shell was anxious not to lose investor confidence (Hoyos et al. 2004a, 2004b).

Prospect theory may also explain why accountants Andersen justified signing off Enron's accounting procedures year after year. Moore et al. (2006) suggest that escalation happened very slowly. In year one the auditors (who, before the Sarbanes-Oxley Act 2002, happened to be selling Enron consultancy as well as auditing) may have decided not to demand that Enron change an accounting proce-dure that was at the margins of legality. Consequently, when the next year Enron pushed its luck, the auditor may have felt the need to justify the previous year's leniency and so ignored it. The following year there is a clear violation of the rules but that too gets ignored because of the perceived need to justify the last two years of leniency. Meanwhile Andersen hopes that Enron will address the problem. Where does it stop? Moore et al. (2006) argue that taking the ethical path involves accepting immediate punishment and disapprobation, whereas the unethical path means incurring only a probability of punishment in the indefinite future. Although prospect theory was originally presented as an alternative to self-justification theory (Whyte 1986), the two are not necessarily at war with one another as decision-makers may be every bit as reluctant to incur loss of esteem as financial loss.

Social drivers of decision error

Very few decisions in complex organizations go awry all at once. Usually there are opportunities to halt a questionable course of action sooner rather than later. Deloitte's lawsuit against the Bank of England for misfeasance over its handling of the closure of the now defunct Bank of Credit and Commerce International (BCCI) began to unravel almost from day one of the trial, yet Deloitte continued with hopeless litigation for almost two years at a cost of tens of millions of pounds and is now being countersued for costs by the Bank of England.

It is unclear what drove Deloitte to persist for so long. Escalation theory would point to the presence of an audience as a potentially powerful driver. For example, experiments have shown that individuals who set budgets in public may quit when the budget is expended even though their economic data clearly suggests that further investment is justified. In debriefings respondents said that having publicly committed themselves to clearly defined limits, they thought it would look good to quit when those limits were reached even though it meant making an economically suboptimal decision (Brockner et al. 1981; see also Brockner and Houser 1986).

An interesting example of audience effects and escalation concerns the so-called dollar auction. Imagine a dollar coin being put up for auction. There is no reserve price and therefore in theory the coin could be acquired for as little as one cent. A special rule, however, attaches to the auction, namely that the second highest bidder pays the bid price. Would you bid in such an auction?

It is probably unwise, as anyone who enters the auction risks becoming trapped in an escalatory spiral. Indeed, Teger (1980) reports that the amounts bid in auctions are frequently well above the face value of the coin. Debriefings suggest that competitive bidding in such auctions is primarily driven by reluctance to lose face in front of an audience. The same phenomenon may be responsible for many of the near suicidal price wars between airlines, supermarkets and petrol stations. Interestingly in theory there is a way out of the dollar auction predicament, for if both parties agree to share their losses early on, they can minimize the financial damage and avoid becoming caught up in an escalatory spiral. In practice it usually becomes a case of 'he who rides a tiger...'.

Another social factor that can drive unwarranted persistence is perceived norms for consistency. Culturally we are conditioned to 'keep right on to the end of the road', to 'try, try and try again' when things go wrong and so forth. Margaret Thatcher's premiership is a prototypical case. Having become personally identified with her government's policy of 'Thatcherism', it became impossible to effect a U-turn when the policy began to meet with hostility from the electorate, particularly as Thatcher herself had declared 'the lady is not for turning'. An added pressure is the western stereotype of the ideal leader as one who is resolute and decisive, that is, makes decisions quickly and sticks to them, whereas leaders who take their time to decide and change direction frequently risk being seen as weak and vacillating.

The missing hero

Social pressure can work in strange ways. A young woman was attacked and raped in the United States. Many people witnessed the attack but no one sent for the police. This singular failure to take responsibility may well have happened because everyone assumed that someone else would act. In other words, the tragedy happened not despite the presence of so many people but *because* of the presence of so many people (Platt 1973; Watzlawick 1993). Such behaviour may also have been driven by the prospect of loss in that contacting the police would have meant not being able to witness the attack and subsequently supply the police with information.

Organizational drivers of escalation

> We've travelled too far, and our momentum has taken over; we move idly towards eternity.
>
> (*Rosencrantz and Guildenstern are Dead,* Stoppard 1967: 90)

Suboptimal decisions can be perpetuated by the sheer weight of the organization itself – sometimes without organizations realizing it until it is too late to change direction. One reason why organizations may end up 'drifting idly towards eternity' is that organizations can become caught up in an escalatory spiral not so much because of a deliberate decision to mount the proverbial tiger but more as a result of inaction.

Escalation that results from inaction is sometimes referred to as entrapment. To be more precise, entrapment refers to situations where time rather than money is the key form of investment. In an experiment respondents were invited to solve a crossword puzzle. The incentive was a cash prize to the first person to successfully complete the task. As part of the experiment, respondents were told that a dictionary that would greatly increase their chances of winning was available and that they were first, second, third etc. in the queue for this valuable resource. In fact, there was no dictionary as the purpose of the experiment was to discover just how long respondents would be prepared to wait for something destined never to arrive! As expected, the researchers discovered that the longer respondents waited for the dictionary, the more likely they were to go on waiting – particularly if they believed they were first or second in the queue (Rubin and Brockner 1975).

In a seminal article, Becker (1960) suggests that entrapment at the individual level results from making 'side-bets', that is, that accumulate over time until eventually it becomes too expensive to change direction. For instance, when an employee is new in a job, pension benefits and other service entitlements may be inconsequential but eventually these side-bets hold individuals in place because it has become too expensive to leave. Likewise, the longer someone remains in a particular career or profession, the harder it becomes to start again.

Entrapment is potentially more invidious than escalation because it happens slowly. For instance, Brockner et al. (1979) observed that persistence with a suboptimal course of action was more pronounced where decisions about continuance could be made passively than when they had to be made actively. Likewise, Drummond (2004) observed how continuity can destroy a small business as owners discover a formula for success but fail to make necessary adaptations as times change. To make matters worst we tend to be more sensitive to relative than absolute magnitudes of change (Kahneman and Tversky 1979, 1982). In other words we may be slow to realize the danger of entrapment because we notice say the latest drop in turnover or the latest half point fall of an index rather than the totality of decline over the years.

Organizations and entrapment

Organizations, like individuals, are vulnerable to entrapment but they face additional dimensions of complexity. Entrapment happens because the cost salience of *not* doing something is initially low (Brockner et al. 1979). Yet by the time the opportunity costs of not doing something dawn on decision-makers, it may be too late. It is easy to understand why individuals make poor decisions, but why do sophisticated organizations employing legions of analysts to scan the environment and report upon threats and opportunities make the same mistake?

Part of the corpus of organization theory suggests that organizations become entrapped not so much despite their sophistication but rather because of it. In this view organizations do not observe their environments but create them, and then end up acting as if their creations are forcing them to act in that way, which ultimately they are! Moreover, their creations are likely to be self-serving rather than utility maximizing.

To understand why this may be so, we need to step back and consider how organizations make decisions. The decision-making process can be seen as beginning with a problem. The trouble is problems do not arrive neatly labelled and objectively defined but are shaped by decision-makers who may have conflicting views about the nature of the problem and what, if anything, should be done about it. In other words, organizations may define their problems in a highly subjective manner and the resultant definition may be a poor match to actual reality:

> A problem is an ideological molecule that integrates elements such as values, causal beliefs, terminology and perceptions. Over time people expand one of these molecules to edit out inharmonious elements. Being an ideological element in itself, a problem's label helps to determine which ideological elements fit in. The problem evolves toward an ideal type that matches its label and rational logic, but deviates more and more from immediate realities.
>
> (Starbuck 1983: 94)

The organization may deviate further and further from reality because of the programmes and protocols that organizations use to collect and process information and address problems – known as action generators (e.g. Brown 1978; Drummond 2001; Starbuck 1993; Weick 1979). Action generators reflect what the organization sees as important. They play a critical role in decision-making because they define the rules of relevance.

In other words, action generators constitute a structure not only of selective attention but also one of *inattention* whereby organizations screen out information deemed irrelevant to their immediate focus and interests. The more this type of control is exercised, the narrower will become the gates through which information must pass. This is because the greater the number and level of rules to control input (clean up data, screen out noise) the fewer the premises included and therefore the narrower the range of options perceived as available (Brown 1989; Starbuck 1983; see also Weick 1979, 1985).

Starbuck (1983) cites a company called Facit, which manufactured mechanical calculators – an activity at which it excelled. Facit knew everything there was to know about the business because all of its action generators, that is, methods of environmental scanning, selection of information, recruitment processes, training programmes and so forth, were geared to the perceived 'problem' of maintaining a reputation for excellence in the design and manufacture of mechanical calculators.

Consequently when electronic calculators began to appear, Facit hardly noticed, because the firm's action generators screened out most of the information because it was deemed to be irrelevant. Consequently Facit remained oblivious to this potentially ominous environmental change and continued investing in research and development into improving its mechanical calculators, believing that they had a future:

> Stability tends to occur in the structural facades that legitimate organizations in terms of societal ideologies, while changes appear in behaviours, technologies and environments . . . The stability of programs and relations may bring on revolutionary crises that end in organizational demise.
>
> (Starbuck 1983: 99)

To paraphrase Starbuck, action generators construct realities that match their self-serving assumptions by filtering information and focusing attention (Starbuck 1983: 93). The result is an illusion of control because within the programmed domain everything appears to be working.

The environment that organizations create for themselves within the programmed domain may be conceptualized as a myth (Hedberg and Jonsson 1977). Myths are partial representations of reality that represent the dominant view about what should be done. All myths are partly true and therefore partly untrue. Myths have their uses as they can prevent organizations from overreacting to minor environmental turbulence. The trouble is self-serving myths can prove enormously resilient even when flatly contradicted by reality. Facit, for example, firmly believed that consumers would be slow to switch to electronic calculators. IBM proved slow to accept the demise of mainframe computing. Kodak ignored the advent of digital photography. More recently US based energy company Enron created and believed in a myth of an immensely profitable firm until a catastrophic fall in share price meant that the myth could no longer adequately account for reality (e.g. Eichenwald 2005).

Starbuck (1983) suggests that the molecules become so big and crystalline that managers are unable to dissolve received views of reality – one reason, suggests Brown (1978), why cuckolded spouses are usually the last to hear of their partner's infidelity, and why rulers remain oblivious to the impending rebellion until it is too late:

> Organizations facing crimes demonstrate this. The organization finds it hard even to notice that anything is amiss, but symptoms do eventually attract attention and percolate up to the top management who attribute the symptoms to a temporary environmental disturbance.
>
> (Starbuck 1983: 96)

A ruling myth holds sway against competing myths while ever it can account for a sufficient portion of reality. In this view a crisis does not create a problem so much as *expose* one because it means that myth and reality no longer match. For example, the disastrous explosion at Chernobyl finally destroyed the myth that nuclear power is safe (e.g. Ross and Staw 1993).

Values and purposes

Staw and Ross (1987) suggest that organizations are most likely to persist with a questionable course of action if it is identified with the values and purposes of the firm. They cite the case of Pan Am, which sold its profitable businesses in hotels and real estate and reinvested the money to support its loss-making aviation business. By the same token, when falling sales began to contradict the myth that mechanical calculators had a future, Facit responded by selling off the profitable parts of the firm like its typewriter manufacturing business and reinvested the proceeds in mechanical calculators. It was plainly irrational but Facit's management understood mechanical calculators whereas electronics was a foreign country (Starbuck 1983). Entrepreneurs are more likely to sell businesses they have bought and keep businesses they have started, even if the former are profitable and the latter are making a loss.

Feeding the myth: organizational politics

Continuing the allusion to tigers, two friends were sharing a tent when a tiger arrived on the scene. One man reached for his shoes. The other said, 'It's no good, you'll never outrun the tiger.' The friend replied, 'I don't need to outrun the tiger, I only need to outrun you.'

Of course both eventually got eaten by the tiger. The moral of the story is that cooperation (helping each other up a tree) usually achieves more than competition. Ghoshal and Moran (1996) use this anecdote in their influential critique of transaction cost theory where they argue that the real purpose of organizations is not to limit opportunism as discussed earlier but that organizations exist because, through cooperation and coordinated effort, they can achieve what would be impossible for an individual working alone.

The trouble is, in practice, the pursuit of vested interest can undermine cooperation to the detriment of the organization. For instance, actors may be selective when it comes to sharing information in order to present themselves in the best possible light. Politically adroit actors may sense which way the wind is blowing and tell their hierarchical superiors what they want to hear rather than risk their careers by contradicting the ruling myth. Dean Rusk, former US Secretary of State, had a formula for political survival in situations of high uncertainty: 'To endure and survive, to keep playing a mediocre hand rather than risk all for a better one, and to stand around for greater achievement another day' (Kramer 1998: 254). Likewise former presidential adviser Arthur Schlesinger kept to himself his reservations about the plans to invade Cuba in 1961 – a venture that culminated in the Bay of Pigs fiasco. Afterwards Schlesinger said, 'My feelings of guilt were tempered by the knowledge that a course of objection would have accomplished little save to gain me a name as a nuisance' (Kramer 1998: 255, citing Arthur Schlesinger, italics removed).

Vested interests can combine to create and defend myths. For example, in the early 1960s system-built housing programmes in the UK were propelled along by various coalitions who saw something in it for themselves. Politicians saw it as a way of fulfilling electoral promises to build more homes to relieve a housing crisis. Architects, surveyors and construction companies saw a way to make money. All doubts about the structural integrity of the buildings were swept aside. System-built housing was 'what should be done' until the fatal gas explosion at Ronan Point in 1968 destroyed the myth.

Sense-making

Of course, until decision-makers can make sense of something in the first place, there is no decision to make (Weick 1995). Decision-makers may succumb to error if their expectations are inconsistent with present reality. In a nutshell, the literature on sense-making suggests that expectations *are* powerful realities. In other words, once we formulate an explanation for something, rather than adjust our explanation as new information emerges, we tend to process and filter new information to fit the existing framework (e.g. Watzlawick 1976; Weick 1995).

The explosion and leaking of toxic gas at Bhopal in 1984 that killed over 2000 people and injured thousands more could have been averted but for a failure of sense-making. Supervisors understood that 90 per cent of the variances in gauges were caused by fluctuations in electricity supply. Consequently, on the night of the explosion when gauges surged to danger, the information was ignored because it was assumed to represent nothing out of the ordinary (Weick 1988; see also the gripping account by Lapierre and Moro 1997).

Likewise, in 1981 Price Waterhouse reviewed the books of the Bank of Credit and Commerce International. It was an opportunity to detect fraud a decade before BCCI was compulsorily closed down with a $1 billion 'hole' in the balance sheet: '*BCCI was a gigantic hall of mirrors; money that didn't exist, customers who didn't exist, money that went round in circles, money that vanished, and money that simply popped up out of nowhere*' (Financial Times 1991: 42, italics in original). Price Waterhouse uncovered irregularities but mistakenly attributed deliberate manipulations to fictitiously inflate income to 'Incompetence, errors made by unsophisticated amateurs venturing into a highly technical and sophisti-cated market' (Bingham 1992: 44; see also Arnold and Sikka 2001).

The official inquiry into BCCI's ignominious end noted that Price Waterhouse was also acting as consultants to BCCI (for example, advising BCCI on how to avoid attracting UK tax liabilities) while the state was relying upon it to monitor the bank's activities, thus perhaps implying that Price Waterhouse was more lenient than it might otherwise have been. Yet it is also possible that Price Waterhouse simply could not believe what it was seeing, that is, 'Bank of Crooks and Cocaine International'.

Moreover, once we formulate an explanation for something incredible, blind spots can develop. Weick (1993) cites the case of a team of firefighters told to expect a 'ten o'clock' fire, that is, one that would be under control by ten o'clock next morning. In fact the fire was much more serious. As the team approached the blaze by helicopter, however, they rationalized what they saw on the ground to fit the expectation of a 'ten o'clock' fire. Consequently they were hopelessly ill prepared (psychologically and operationally) to fight the blaze and most of the crew were killed as the flames suddenly overtook them. In 1975 two planes collided on the runway at Tenerife airport, killing 512 people in the worst disaster in aviation history. There were many indirect causes of the disaster such as the backlog of delayed planes waiting to take off, tired and stressed crews and poor visibility. The immediate cause may have been the pilot of one the planes hearing what he was expecting to hear, that is, 'OK take-off' when the air traffic controller actually said, 'OK standby for take-off'. In addition, the air traffic controller may also have heard what he expected to hear, namely, 'We are at take off position,' when the pilot actually said, 'We are taking off' (Weick 1990).

When we encounter something that seems incredible we may refuse to believe it:

> Sensemaking is tested to the extreme when people encounter an event whose occurrence is so implausible that they hesitate to report it, for fear they will not be believed. In essence, these people think to themselves, it can't be, therefore, it isn't.
>
> (Weick 1995: 1)

According to Weick, this is why battered child syndrome and other forms of child abuse went unrecognized for so long. Self-censorship may also explain why no one suspected the family doctor named Harold Shipman of murder. Pharmacists were well aware of his unusual prescribing habits. For years, fellow doctors countersigned an astonishing number of death certificates. It was only when Shipman forged the will of one of his victims that a relative reported her suspicions to the police. Yet initially the police refused to believe her. We will never know how many of his elderly patients Shipman killed, because he committed suicide in prison, but it may have been more than 200.

Organizations are not immune from exercising self-censorship. One of the most chilling passages of the report into events of 9/11 entitled *The System was Blinking Red* is peppered with reports of suspicious incidents such as foreigners known to possess jihadist connections paying in cash for flight training on Pan Am's Boeing 747 flight simulators who clearly had no intention of becoming commercial pilots and of persons identified as 'major-league killers' passing money around. The report depicts intelligence officials (ignorant of the flight training reports) searching CIA databases for information about the movements of those major-league killers and discovering that they held US visas; then re-examining old cables trying to 'figure out what those cables meant' (National Commission on Terrorist Attacks 2004: 267) and waiting for information from other departments in an effort to unearth information about possible terrorist connections knowing that 'something bad was definitely up' (National Commission on Terrorist Attacks 2004: 268). Their efforts were unavailing because of the void between foreign and domestic intelligence agencies:

> The foreign intelligence agencies were watching overseas, alert to foreign threats to US interests there. The domestic agencies were waiting for

evidence of . . . a threat from sleeper cells within the United States. No one was looking for a foreign threat to domestic targets. The threat that was coming was not from sleeper cells. It was foreign – but from foreigners who had infiltrated into the United States.

(National Commission on Terrorist Attacks 2004: 263)

Given time, the intelligence agencies might have assembled enough pieces of the jigsaw to fill that void but by late August 2001, 'Time was short, and running out' (National Commission on Terrorist Attacks 2004: 277).

What occurred is similar to the failure of sense-making that preceded the Three Mile Island disaster where the warning lights were blinking but no one understood their meaning because of the interaction of multiple failures not in direct operational sequence. Moreover, to paraphrase Perrow (1984: 31), if anyone had a hunch about what was happening they failed to pause long enough to examine the implications of their intuition. Clearly in the case of 9/11 the action generators had been designed for a bygone era. Even so, it is conceivable that if it had crossed an analyst's mind that terrorists might be about to use civil aircraft in an attack, they might well have exercised self-censorship – 'It can't be'.

11 'A million bucks a day'

As each day went on, and my requests continued to be met, the explanation dawned on me: they wanted to believe it was all true.

(Leeson 1997: 217)

Leeson spent Christmas 1994 in Ireland. He decided not to return to Barings but his wife Lisa persuaded him to reconsider and remain at least until the end of February 1995 to collect his £450,000 bonus payment (Leeson 1997). There was a problem waiting for Leeson when he returned. SIMEX had written to Simon Jones saying the margin account for customer positions was apparently under-funded by $100 million, and that, contrary to the rules, Barings was apparently financing margin payments on a customer account. Both allegations were true. Leeson had manipulated the accounts to reduce the amount of margin called by SIMEX (a sum that ultimately escalated to over £250 million). Moreover, Barings was indeed financing a customer – itself. Luckily for Leeson, Simon Jones did not inform Geoff Broadhurst, Barings' Group Finance Director, about the letter. Instead he passed it to Leeson and demanded an explanation.

Leeson played a cool hand. He returned the letter to Jones with a scribbled note, 'Let's discuss it later' (Leeson 1997: 214). Leeson subsequently claimed that SIMEX was getting confused, 'banging on' (Leeson 1997: 215) about intra-day trading limits and muddling client and house positions. He offered to draft a reply. The reply was a convoluted account of excess funds held in various accounts being used for funding, and time zone differences as explaining the apparent funding of customer positions.

Shortly afterwards another letter arrived from SIMEX, this time alleging improper segregation and computation of client funds. Since the letter also questioned Barings' ability to meet margin calls, Jones had to refer it to London. An explanatory note drafted by Leeson accompanied the letter, suggesting that SIMEX was becoming confused. London soon lost interest in the issue. A fortnight later on 10 February, Barings assured SIMEX that it understood its financial obligations and would always honour them:

It is the policy of Baring Investment Bank Group to ensure that risks of all kinds, including exposure to exceptional intra-day calls for settlement variation and advance margin are managed actively. All risks are monitored daily ... and reported to the Asset and Liability Committee. Immediate action is taken to correct situations where a group is over-exposed to a particular risk.

(Summary of Evidence, Secretary of State
versus certain Barings' Directors)

'This guy ... is making a million bucks a day'

Contrary to Barings' claim about active management of margin, London was still in 'the awkward position of having to transfer amounts of the order of $10 million with just a few hours notice and without any clear idea of who is being lent the cash' (Secretary of State versus Gamby). In November 1994, Ian Hopkins, Barings' newly appointed Head of Risk, discovered that Barings was advancing margin for customer trading without making proper credit checks. 'Our efforts on credit are more form than substance' (Board of Banking Supervision 1995: 112), he wrote in a confidential memo to Norris. Norris was not impressed.

Hopkins asked for more staff to review controls. Norris, at the instigation of Broadhurst, refused the request. Hopkins then tried to investigate Leeson's unusual profits, fearing that Leeson was breaking trading limits. 'It is becoming clear that our systems and control culture are distinctly flaky' (Board of Banking Supervision 1995: 120), he warned Norris. Following vigorous protests from Leeson, supported by Baker and Waltz, Hopkins was forced to retract, saying that it was a routine inquiry. In early February, Hopkins was sacked from the Asset and Liability Committee (ALCO, chaired by Norris). His place was taken by Baker.

By now, however, it was obvious that Hopkins' concerns were by no means unfounded. In early January 1995 the external auditors Coopers and Lybrand (Singapore) telephoned Leeson about a problem. 'This was the call that would kill me,' said Leeson (1996: 224). The auditor said, 'I need to ask you about a receivable from SIMEX which I can't trace. It's quite a big sum: 7.78 billion yen' (Leeson 1997: 224).

Leeson said something vague about the computer system and promised to get back to the auditor. For the next two days Leeson avoided returning the auditor's telephone calls. Then Simon Jones confronted him: 'What's all this about 7.78 billion yen?' Jones appeared to be more worried about how London would react. Leeson said that he had sold a £50 million option 'over the counter' (OTC) to a firm of brokers named Spear Leeds and Kellogg (SLK) and forgotten to collect the money.

> 'It's a nightmare ... It was an OTC trade last month which was incorrectly booked. The auditors are giving me a rough time over it.'
> 'They're a pain in the arse,' said Jones
>
> (Leeson 1997: 225)

Coopers then sent a status report to London about the alleged transaction:

> There is a JPY 7.7 billion ... trade receivable from a third party – Spear Leeds & Kellogg ... This represents refund of margin deposited with SLG

[*sic*] for an over-the-counter Nikkei option which expired on 30 December 1994. The amount is still outstanding. We are awaiting confirmation of the year end balance ... We are informed that collectability of the said JPY 7.7 billion is not envisaged to be a problem. Also the counteracting party with SLG is Barings Securities Ltd ('BSL') and that SLG is an ongoing client and is credit worthy.

(Summary of Evidence, Secretary of State
versus certain Barings' Directors)

The report caused uproar in London. On 31 January 1995 Tony Hawes sent a cc. mail to Leeson and Jones quoting the status report, adding: 'To us here this looks a very muddled and strange comment. Please phone as possible to discuss' (Board of Banking Supervision 1995: 159).

Leeson stalled, saying it was the Chinese New Year. Meanwhile he scribbled a note of explanation to Jones. It was complete nonsense but Leeson calculated upon Jones being too embarrassed to ask him to explain it (Leeson 1997: 304). The note continued: 'As trade was to have no impact, referral was not made, so blame me! ... There are obviously a lot of errors that I can be hung on, to which I take full responsibility' (Leeson 1997: 304). Jones was worried as Leeson had no authority to conduct such a trade. He assumed that it 'must have been approved by London' (Ministry for Finance, Singapore 1995: 119), but never attempted to compare notes. Had he done so, he would have discovered that no one in London knew anything about the alleged sale.

Initially there were no fewer than six versions of the so-called 'SLK transaction' circulating in London. It was clear from the start, however, that Barings was owed £50 million. Moreover, it was unclear how it had been funded. The settlements office in London had no record of it. Might it have been funded by excess margin? Was Barings failing to keep accounting records in accordance with section 221 of the Companies Act 1985? Brenda Granger, Manager of Futures and Options Settlement, suggested to Tony Gamby, Settlements Director, that someone should telephone SLK for confirmation. Gamby said 'No' – the story was too confused and besides, no one was pressing them to act. Gamby also instructed Tony Railton, Futures and Options Settlement Clerk based in London, not to involve himself in the matter when he visited Singapore:

I was told not to get involved in it because it was nothing to do with me. It was purely a case of something had been done by a senior member of staff and because of my [relatively junior] level I was told not to get involved in it because – well, for one thing it was none of my business really.

(Evidence given by Tony Railton in Secretary of
State versus Gamby)

Senior staff discovered it was none of their business either.

On 2 February 1995 Tony Hawes spoke to Mary Waltz. Waltz said it was a 'booking error where we actually had cash out the door', adding that if the payment did relate to margin the underlying trade must have been 'enormous' (Secretary of State versus Baker). When Hawes tried to probe this 'booking error' Waltz warned him against asking 'time consuming or difficult questions', adding that she did not want 'every morning to be a giant investigation into Nick's life', because it was:

> The wrong thing to do to this guy who I suspect has done nothing terribly wrong is just to have interrogations every morning ... when he is making a million bucks a day ... There is just too much interrogation of what is basically a pretty sound business.
>
> (Board of Banking Supervision 1995: 130)

Hawes then approached Bax for help. 'Nick [Leeson] is under a lot of strain at the moment,' Bax replied. 'Perhaps it would be better if I questioned Nick ... rather than you ... to play the thing down' (Board of Banking Supervision 1995: 133). At Bax's instigation, Broadhurst persuaded the external auditors to omit the incident from their management letter as it would be detrimental for Barings to come to SIMEX's attention again.

The auditors, anxious to finalize the accounts, were pressing Leeson for documentary proof of the alleged trade. In fact there was no sum of money owing. The £50 million represented part of Leeson's losses from his illicit options trading. Leeson set about manufacturing the requisite 'proof'. He typed a letter of authority and then forged Baker's signature. He then retrieved an old letter signed by Richard Hogan, managing director of SLK, cut out his signature and affixed it to two forged letters. One letter dated 1 October 1994 purported to be an order for the option Leeson claimed to have sold. The other letter, dated 30 September 1994, supplied confirmation of payment from SLK. Leeson then instructed a clerk to transfer £50 million from an account held with Citibank into another account, and obtain a statement to make it look as if the debt had been paid before reversing the transaction.

Leeson then handed the documentation to the auditors except for the letter from SLK confirming payment, as it had to come directly from SLK to the auditors. He dispatched the two-page letter from his home fax machine. Both sheets bore an imprint made by his fax machine, 'From Nick and Lisa'. Despite this unmistakable flaw, next day the auditors cleared the accounts.

Now that the money had apparently been paid, the tension subsided. Norris and Bax called it a 'back office glitch', 'a booking error' and a 'non-transaction' (Board of Banking Supervision 1995: 135). On 13 February Norris (preoccupied with seemingly worse settlement problems in Mexico) reported an 'operational error' in Singapore to the Management Committee. The report was received without comment. Leeson said:

> Nobody asked me outright how on earth I had arranged for the 7.78 billion yen to leave Barings. I knew from my experience ... that when it came down to detail no senior managers actually wanted to get their hands dirty and investigate the numbers ... And they never dared ask me any basic questions since they were afraid of looking stupid about not understanding futures and options.
>
> (Leeson 1997: 240)

Meanwhile, it looked as if some good would come from the incident. On 3 February 1995 Bax wrote to Baker and Tony Gamby saying: 'As you know recent incidents have highlighted the current operational weakness of our SIMEX business and an urgent need for a new approach.' The letter (sent by fax) then suggests immediate segregation:

> With immediate effect split Nick's role so that he is no longer responsible for settlement functions. In the past Nick has been willing to do that but now appreciates that the demands on him are too much to perform both tasks satisfactorily.'
>
> (Fay 1996: 170)

In the event, nothing happened.

That was not quite the end of the matter. On 7 February Hawes (assisted by Hopkins) produced a list of questions for Leeson to answer. Baker was furious. He told Norris that Hawes was ineligible to investigate because it was his fault for releasing margin in the first place (Secretary of State versus Baker). Baker also wanted to protect his star trader. 'I felt it was my responsibility to offer Nick a first line protection against this thing' (Evidence given by Baker in Secretary of State versus Baker).

Baker sought and received an assurance from Bax that Hawes would not be allowed to question Leeson. In fact Hawes did meet with Leeson and, realizing the inconsistencies in Leeson's story, subsequently circulated a second list of questions to ALCO. (Hawes was then recalled to London on a separate matter.) On 14 February Hawes faxed a reminder to Simon Jones about his second list of questions. Jones replied that Leeson was dealing with it. James Bax scribbled the following message to Jones on his copy of the fax: 'Simon: Can we not get Nick out of this loop? It makes more sense for you to take on TH [Tony Hawes]' (Secretary of State versus Baker).

'Nobody else to ask'

Leeson had staked everything on the Nikkei index remaining virtually stable at 19,200. On 17 January 1995 an earthquake struck Japan, killing 3000 people and destroying 25,000 buildings. Trade and communications were severely disrupted and the index plummeted:

> The risk inherent in taking a position of this nature is a sudden and unexpected move in the market. The Kobe earthquake caused precisely that, as concerns about its long term effects on the Japanese economy and the continuing growth of the Yen caused the Nikkei index to fall sharply below 17,000 towards the end of February 1995.
>
> (Board of Banking Supervision 1995: 70)

The resultant wave of selling forced Leeson to buy massive quantities in a desperate effort to force the index to rise.

For instance, on 20 January 1995 Leeson bought 8000 contracts for account 88888. The following Monday, 23 January 1995, the market opened 30 points up and drifted upwards for about an hour. Then, it suddenly fell by 1175 points. Leeson's reported revenues for the day were a stunning £3.3 million. The reality was a £100 million loss in a single day.

On Wednesday 25 January, the Nikkei recovered slightly to around 18,060 prompting Leeson to double his bet. He told Gueler he was acting for a customer determined to corner the market and arbitraging on the back of 'Customer X's relentless buying. 'The guy must be insane' (Gapper and Denton 1996: 285), said Gueler. Peter Norris asked for a breakdown of Leeson's extraordinary profits. Ron Baker passed the request to Mary Waltz:

> Ron called me … He said: 'Look, do something on analysis of the p&l for Monday [23 January].' I was quite stressed with him. I said, 'I am really busy. Can Ian [Hopkins] not do it, or somebody in risk control?' [He said]: 'Just do something for George [Maclean] and Peter [Norris].' … I did a quick thing based on conversations with those guys, Benjamin [Fuchs, a BSJ trader], Fernando [Gueler] and Nick [Leeson] of what I thought happened in those days. I scratched it down for Ron and sent it to him … I think there was possibly one other conversation with Ron about it. He said to me: 'Do not worry about it. That is an offer. Nobody needs anything.'
>
> (Secretary of State versus Baker np)

In a covering fax to Mr Baker, Waltz describes her report as 'very poor'. Baker added a few words and then passed it to Norris. No more was heard of it (Secretary of State versus Baker np).

'They wanted to believe it was all true …'

By now Barings had paid out over £221 million in margin calls, of which less than £30 million matched known customer positions. In a cc. mail to Leeson dated 3 January 1995, Railton asked, 'How do you come to the USD funding figure on a daily basis. A lot of figures do not appear to move very often' (Secretary of State versus Gamby).

Since Barings' settlements office understood it was merely transferring payments internally as distinct from transferring money to a customer account, staff were less concerned about controlling the flow of margin to Singapore than they might otherwise have been. Even so, settlements required details of the underlying trades giving rise to margin calls so that it could match margin to trades.

Having tried unsuccessfully to obtain information from Leeson, Hawes asked Bax for an 'identification of the causes of the very large and consistent requirements for funding from London', and a 'confirmation that house margin is provided in the correct fashion' (Secretary of State versus Gamby). Bax merely passed the memo to Jones, who in turn asked Leeson to reply. The response left Hawes no wiser. Moreover, Leeson's US$ margin requests were not what the settlements office was accustomed to receiving, as they were always in round numbers. For example, the split between client and house margin funding was usually 50:50 or 60:40 or 40:60. Railton subsequently said he was almost certain Leeson was concocting the figures because they were too neat. However, he assumed that Leeson was trying to hide administrative chaos. Granger too refers to awaiting the breakdown from her 'buddy' Nick, 'once they creatively allocate the numbers' (Secretary of State versus Gamby).

Brenda Granger was often kept waiting:

> [Mrs Granger's] concern was that Nick a lot of the time would not return calls or we could not get in touch with him, and the girls out there could not give us any information on how things worked ... For instance, in the morning we would call up Nick and would have to speak to Nick for an estimate of how much money he would require in dollars because the girls could never answer our queries ... Then in the evening when the day's work was finished they would tell us how much dollars they wanted, that could be completely wrong. Obviously that is not very good, when you have no idea of being able to reconcile it.
>
> (Evidence given by Tony Railton in Secretary of State
versus certain Barings' Directors)

The Board of Banking Supervision concluded that if Hawes or Granger had attempted to use the information supplied by Leeson, 'They would have discovered that it was meaningless' (Board of Banking Supervision 1995: 101). In fact, they already knew it was meaningless since the joke in London was that anyone could send their mother out to Singapore and get a better idea of what Leeson's funding requests meant, 'since Nick is so busy now' (Secretary of State versus Gamby np).

On 25 January, Brenda Granger wrote to Hawes: 'Below the funding breakdown as received from our pals in Singapore. Please be advised that it is not completely accurate' (Secretary of State versus Gamby). Granger's doubts were well founded. For instance in early February 1995, Leeson made $48 million margin call. He instructed the clerk to give a breakdown of 50:50 then changed his mind. 'Actually make it 60:40, we did 50:50 yesterday' (Leeson 1997: 274).

When Hawes subsequently questioned Baker about Leeson's escalating margin calls, the two men crossed swords again. 'My numbers were unreal. I knew that,' says Leeson. 'In London they were beginning to think they were unreal as well' (Leeson 1997: 218). Baker was not interested; he thought Hawes should be doing his utmost to find the money to support Leeson's trading, not raising obstacles. 'That was a bad relationship,' said Norris ... '[and] a very important one' (Board of Banking Supervision 1995: 98).

Finding the money to support Leeson's trading was becoming a problem. After the earthquake, Leeson's margin calls were stretching Barings' finances to breaking point. On 25 January Hawes reported to ALCO that Barings had almost broken its overdraft limit with Citibank. The minutes of the meeting state:

> AJDH [Mr Hawes] reported that without a booking error we would have broken our day-light margin call limit with Citibank ... The Committee noted

the general lack of and inaccuracy about margin calls received from Singapore and decided to discuss who should be responsibility [sic] for issues of this nature.

(Secretary of State versus Baker)

Later that day Baker telephoned Leeson informing him of ALCO's instruction not to increase his positions and if possible reduce them to give Barings a breathing space. 'The old farts want you to unwind the position a little,' Baker told Leeson (Leeson 1997: 171). Leeson's trading promptly doubled. 'Ron's going to get mad at me, but there was some good money in it' Leeson told Waltz (Leeson 1997: 173).

'Ron' was indeed concerned, 'I know it's a hedged position ... but people are beginning to talk,' he told Leeson (Leeson 1997: 265).

Specifically the information before ALCO on 26 January 1995 listed the following increases in Leeson's positions:

Nikkei 225: increased from US$564.7 million to US$1,545.9 million
JGB increased from US$4,973.9 million to US$6,839.3 million
Euroyen increased from US$481.3 million to US$601.8 million.

Already rumours were beginning to circulate in the financial markets in the Far East about Barings becoming overexposed to a customer who might not be able to meet margin calls. Anxious not to fuel those rumours by being seen to falter, ALCO discussed how it would ensure sufficient funds would be available to meet sudden intra-day margin calls and the possibility of arranging additional overdraft facilities. Baker said that as they are making a profit, it would be worth it. No one asked why Leeson's positions had suddenly doubled. Nor did anyone worry about the risks of overexposure, as ALCO assumed Leeson's positions were matched. Recall that matched positions exist where a contract to buy is matched with a contract to sell. Norris, who chaired ALCO's meetings, said: 'Discussion ... started with a reconfirmation that all our positions were fully matched. That premise was never doubted ...' (Board of Banking Supervision 1996: 137).

As regards market rumour, ALCO assumed that people were beginning to talk out of ignorance. The minutes of the meeting on 26 January record:

It is important that the market does not misinterpret our positions. PN [Mr Norris] reported that several people had reported receiving calls asking what was happening ... The major cause of rumours about our positions is that open interest on the Osaka exchange is given by a member, which does not happen on SIMEX, leading people to assume we have a significant long position.

(Summary of Evidence, Secretary of State versus certain Barings' Directors)

In other words, ALCO was assuming that since one exchange published trading positions and the other did not, the market was seeing only part of the equation.

'It's bad'

In the last week of January 1995, Leeson's reported profits for that week were $9 million whereas his colleagues in Japan lost $1 million. In a conversation with Sajeed Sacranie, Peter Norris's personal assistant, Baker explained Leeson's results as resulting from 'a mesh of volumes in the market ... a perfect trading environment for Nick to work in.'

> 'Huge liquidity and gaps,' said Sacranie.
> Then Sacranie asks, 'Are you comfortable that he didn't take any specific or directional risks during the day?'
> Baker replied, 'I trust the guy a fair bit. It's really hard for me to say. I think ... he just sees opportunities that are phenomenal, and he just takes them'.
>
> (Gapper and Denton 1996: 289)

Privately Baker was less sanguine as Leeson continued to defy instructions not to increase positions:

> 'It's bad,' he said in a telephone call to Waltz.
> 'It's very bad,' Waltz agreed ... 'I really don't know how it happened. Nick and I had spoken about how he was going to be cool ... and then there was a flurry of activity on Wednesday.'
>
> (Secretary of State versus Baker)

Waltz then tells Baker: 'the rumour about us is that we have a customer who has got big margin calls and what if they can't make the margin calls? And Barings is in trouble for that' (Secretary of State versus Baker). Waltz continues: 'He is settlement, he is cash management and he is the trader, and there's a problem, because there's nobody else to call but him about it' (Secretary of State versus Baker).

Undaunted, Waltz again asked Leeson why he had not cut positions as instructed. Leeson claimed that Barings would lose $1 million by selling rapidly: prices on SIMEX would fall faster than those on Osaka because Singapore always overreacts and that is how Barings has made money all along. The explanation made no sense to Waltz or Baker. They tried to call Leeson back but he had disappeared for the weekend.

In mid-February Norris flew to Singapore. He met with Leeson on 15 February. Earlier that day, Leeson had altered the accounts, making a fictitious purchase of 7000 contracts, 745 points below market price. This created a paper gain of £170 million, which would be reversed out tomorrow. Although by now this was routine practice for Leeson, he was so worried that Norris would quiz him about this and other transactions that he was physically sick before the meeting. He need not have worried. The meeting lasted forty minutes but Norris was on the telephone for most of the time. Norris asked Leeson a few general questions about the positions he was running and whether he was happy with them and left it at that. The short attention span suited Leeson: 'So easy to tell everyone not to worry because … Peter Norris knew all about it' (Leeson 1997: 277).

'Customer X'

Around 15 February a director of the bank named Diarmid Kelly began hearing rumours that Barings was seriously overexposed in Singapore. Kelly telephoned Baker to ascertain who Barings was dealing with and to ask Baker to investigate whether the positions were matched or open. Baker rang back half an hour later to confirm that Barings was long 20,076 futures in Osaka. Kelly then asked him if they were short of the same amount in SIMEX. Baker offered to come round with Waltz to explain the situation. Within minutes, however, Kelly was back on the phone seeking definite confirmation as Morgan Stanley and Goldman Sachs were warning their customers to be careful about using Barings as a counterparty. Baker stalled, saying that commercially sensitive information would leak to the market. Kelly then pulled rank, reminding Baker that he is asking, as a member of MACO, 'who the customers are that we are dealing with' (Gapper and Denton 1996: 316, italics in original).

Baker identified three big players, plus a 'strange guy' (Gapper and Denton 1996: 316), 'Customer X', Leeson's mystery customer. Kelly then asks Baker why this 'strange guy' is playing so heavily. Baker says something about hedge funds trying to go short on volatility. They then proceed to discuss risks. Baker tells Kelly (wrongly) that Barings collects margin from customers before making payments to SIMEX, adding that if Morgan Stanley and other competitors were doing as much business in SIMEX as Barings, their profiles would be similar. 'But they can't get in there and they'd love to be in there' (Gapper and Denton 1996: 318).

The explanation satisfies Kelly, who concludes:

> 'The only risk is a funding risk, whereby for some reason or another because of some cock-up in settlements … we haven't called the margin off clients,' said Kelly, putting his finger on exactly the reason why Barings was about to collapse.
>
> (Gapper and Denton 1996: 317)

Meanwhile Leeson's positions continued rising. On 17 February 1995 Baker telephoned Leeson, threatening to 'come down there personally and sort you out' (Gapper and Denton 1995: 319) if positions are not immediately reduced. Leeson shuffled accounts to appear compliant. Next day Waltz spoke with Gueler, saying she understood how Leeson felt at being instructed to cut positions, but they were at capacity. Gueler replies: 'I'm not sure we're at capacity, so much as credibility capacity. We need to prove that it's OK' (Gapper and Denton 1996: 321).

> Gueler then read out the latest long positions and counter-positions taken by other houses lining up against Barings. 'What does that mean?' said Waltz. 'Nothing, I guess.'

'Yeah. They all got short,' said Gueler.
'Yeah. Pretty funny', said Waltz.

(Gapper and Denton 1996: 320)

'Plain rubbish'

On 28 December 1994, Railton emailed Granger about Leeson's margin requests:

> We want to keep a much tighter grip on USD figures. We need to be able to justify why [BFS] wants a certain amount of USD on a particular day ... The best case scenario is that Nick is calling for the right USD but is changing the wrong figures on his breakdown spreadsheet. Worst case is that it's plain rubbish.

(Secretary of State versus Gamby)

In early February 1995, Hawes and Railton travelled to Singapore to try to remedy the chronic and serious reconciliation problem. More specifically, their brief was to:

> Understand the SIMEX exchange, its rules, and that would obviously encompass the reasons Singapore were asking for US dollars. So I was out there really ... to understand the whole thing, and then give them a better way of reporting the funds back.

(Evidence given by Tony Railton in Secretary
of State versus Gamby)

Transparency was the last thing Leeson wanted. He directed Railton to examining intra-day funding requirements which SIMEX were questioning – 'a nicely complicated subject' (Leeson 1997: 251). Leeson also distracted Railton with games of tennis and seductive accounts of the expatriate lifestyle awaiting him if he obtained his hoped-for posting to Singapore.

Distractions notwithstanding, Railton soon realized that the breakdown between customer and house accounts was indeed meaningless and that Leeson was merely instructing the clerk to change figures to make up the total. Still Railton did not suspect malfeasance. He thought Leeson was trying to hide the chaos in the back office. Railton's problem was that when he reconciled the margin payments with the known trading, there was a definite £95 million shortfall. 'If you close out [sell up] all these positions there is absolutely no way on God's earth that you could return all the yen' (Fay 1996: 188).

This gap was caused by account 88888, which Railton had not counted because he had no knowledge of it. Railton said: 'Half the stuff I had been advised on as to how the spread sheet worked did not work ... The project was becoming more and more complicated the further one went along' (Fay 1996: 189). On 17 February, after struggling to make sense of Leeson's accounts for a fortnight, Railton reported the shortfall to Brenda Granger, saying he 'thought he must have missed something that Leeson would be able to explain' (Board of Banking Supervision 1995: 10.)

Granger then spoke to Gamby, who instructed Railton to ask Leeson for help. Gamby was busy with (apparently) far worse settlements problems in Barings' overseas offices. Singapore was fourth on his list of priorities:

> I am speaking to somebody on the telephone many thousands of miles away, who is informing me that he does not understand the reconciliation process, but has agreed with Leeson to come in over the week end and work through this with him ... The overall tone is definitely not alarmist and equally significant action is being taken.
>
> (Evidence given by Tony Gamby in Secretary of State versus Gamby)

Railton persisted for another week. In the intervening period a further US$ 169 million was remitted by the London settlements office to Singapore. Of that sum, $110 million was posted in the last two days of Barings' existence.

By now Leeson was proving more elusive than ever. The Nikkei index had fallen to 17,9991 and Leeson was frantically doubling his positions in a final effort to force the index back up, squandering Barings' cash in the process. Account 88888 now held more than 50,000 Nikkei futures and 27,000 JGB futures. Despite Leeson's frantic buying on Thursday 23 February, the Nikkei index dropped another 277 points, costing Barings another £143 million in one day alone.

When the market closed for the day Leeson returned to his office. A fax from Hawes was waiting for him. Hawes was questioning Leeson's $45 million margin call for the previous day and asking why the figure was rising when it should be falling. 'There is something very odd here,' said Hawes (Gapper and Denton 1996: 325). By now Railton had enlisted Jones' help in pinning Leeson down. Jones had seen the fax from Hawes and the three men sat down to discuss it. After a few minutes Leeson left the meeting promising to return.

He never did return. Railton became alarmed and telephoned Gamby. At about four o'clock in the afternoon (London time) of Thursday 25 February, Norris received an unexpected visitor. Gamby had arrived to tell him about the missing money and the missing trader.

12 Analysis of the final weeks

> I believe it is impossible for commercial organizations, let alone banking organiza-
> tions, to prevent frauds starting. The issue really is how long it takes to discover them.
> (Evidence given by Peter Norris to Treasury Committee,
> 10 June 1996: 55)

During its last eight weeks Barings invested millions of pounds in pursuit of non-existent profits and ignored strong warning signs of malfeasance. Those signs included:

- huge and escalating margin calls unsupported by proper paperwork
- Leeson's defiance of instructions not to increase positions
- rumours of impending collapse
- the knowledge that Leeson's roles were completely unsegregated
- the so-called 'SLK transaction'.

The Board of Banking Supervision (1995) concluded that while each of these
warning signs might not have meant much in isolation, taken together they should
have set alarm bells ringing before it was too late. The focal question for analysis
is why Barings failed to take any effective action until the bank was doomed.

Expectations and self-censorship

How much of what was missed during this crucial period can be explained as a
psychological failure of sense-making? Recall that expectations may become
powerful realities (e.g. Weick 1995). Leeson's failure to submit proper accounts
had become habitual. Actors like Brenda Granger and Tony Railton rationalized
such prima facie evidence of malfeasance to fit the expectation of an overworked
trader trying to do two jobs, and giving greater priority to trading than back office
work. They know that Leeson's accounts are 'not completely accurate', 'plain
rubbish' in fact, but it is what they have come to expect, 'since Nick is so busy
now'. Even when 'Nick' submits his final 'strange and muddled' margin call,
there is no immediate alarm, just a polite request to get in touch.

Assumptions are important because they can create myopia. Social scientists
refer to myopia as a focus upon one set of causes and events that can blind us to

other sets of causes and events (e.g. Simons and Chabris 1999). In more collo-quial language, what stops us from solving a problem may not be the problem itself, but the assumptions we make about the nature of the problem. Having tacitly assumed that Leeson's positions are matched, Railton's task inevitably becomes more and more complicated because nothing fits together. Moreover, although Railton can see that there is no possibility 'on God's earth' of returning all the yen as the accounts stand, myopia blinds him to the possibility that the money is gone.

All banks are on their guard against financial irregularities. Rogue traders were by no means unknown in investment banks before Barings collapsed. The differ-ence was the sheer scale of operations as Leeson's activities were off the Richter scale of malfeasance. Recall that individuals may exercise self-censorship in situ-ations that are so extreme as to be almost inconceivable (e.g. Weick 1995). The difficulty with self-censorship as an explanation is that it is almost impossible to prove what went through an actor's mind at a particular point in time. The analyst must therefore proceed with great caution and accept that any observations are bound to be speculative. Even so it is possible to adduce evidence of self-censorship from actors' behaviour. Railton exercises a form of self-censorship by assuming that he is incompetent: he keeps thinking he must have missed something, as evidenced by his initial telephone call to Tony Gamby in London. The call contains no indication of suspicion. Gamby too is oblivious to the possibility of malfeasance. He accepts Railton's explanation as entirely plausible. The frame is finally broken when Leeson mysteriously disappears. Here was something that could not be rationalized to fit the expectations.

Had Barings not collapsed, the external auditors might have done more work on the accounts. Had that happened they might have queried the dubious fax imprint and noticed that the date on one of the letters was a Saturday and that the manag-ing director's signature was in the wrong typeface (Fay 1996: 162). A plausible explanation for not spotting those flaws before clearing the accounts is that the external auditors succumbed to the phenomenon of mean/ends reversal (e.g. Drummond 1998b; Watson 1994). In other words, they were so preoccupied with getting the accounts ready and assembling the requisite paperwork that those activities became an end in themselves, at the expense of reflecting upon the unusual nature of the alleged transaction and what it might imply. Leeson's delib-erate failure to return telephone calls and other stalling tactics also meant that the auditor's timetable for completing the work became increasingly compressed.

Yet the imprint 'From Nick and Lisa' was plainly evident. No checking was required and the auditors could hardly have missed it. Under intense pressure of work, they might simply have assumed that SLK had misrouted the letter and that Leeson had forwarded it. Alternatively, they may have seen the imprint but not *observed* it. Conceivably when the auditors received the fax, the sheer size of the transaction might have provoked self-censorship, 'A fifty-million pound fraud? It can't be, therefore . . .' (Weick 1995).

Latterly Waltz and Hawes had serious if different concerns about Leeson's behaviour. Yet there is no evidence that they suspected for one moment that

Leeson was Barings' mystery customer. Likewise, Kelly assumes that the rumours about Barings being 'bust' are wrong. Perhaps the most extreme form of self-censorship occurs when Geuler and Waltz discuss competitors taking up positions against Barings. Although by then Barings was doomed, the incident is instructive nevertheless because unlike amorphous rumour, here was a concrete development – akin to the woods moving in Shakespeare's *Macbeth*. Both actors are well qualified and experienced professionals yet neither can get beyond 'pretty funny' when discussing developments. They end up dismissing evidence of nemesis as 'nothing I suppose'.

Beyond self-censorship

Self-censorship will take us only so far. Another important factor was Leeson's continuing dominance. Control may be defined as the 'process of specifying preferred states of affairs and revising ongoing processes to reduce the distance from those preferred states' (Etzioni 1968: 688). Leeson was almost completely out of control during those last eight weeks. Reconciliation requirements had been specified as early as 1992 but Leeson ignored them. Nothing was going to force him to comply now. ALCO specified no increase in positions. Leeson's trade doubled. Leeson's dominance is also seen in his control of information and manipulation of time. SIMEX was getting close to exposing Leeson's manipulations; colleagues in London were beginning to think his numbers were unreal. Railton and Hawes were doggedly pursuing him. Sooner or later he would be found out. Leeson used a combination of delay and dissimulation to postpone discovery.

Positive framing also helped Leeson. Evidence suggests that where issues are positively framed (metaphorical bottle is perceived as half-full rather than half-empty) decisions tend to be subject to much less critical scrutiny than where issues are negatively framed (Dunegan 1993) – a point made by Peter Norris afterwards:

> Where a system of reporting is established and becomes consistent and the results reported on are positive, then an organization is not as critically engaged in its review of an activity as it would be if the results are negative.
>
> (Peter Norris, Treasury Committee, 10 June 1996: 51)

When Gueler loses almost £1 million, ALCO demands an explanation. Yet Leeson's alleged £3.3 million profit prompts only superficial enquiry. The spotlight is on Gueler's competence. No one asks whether Leeson's reported revenues might be too good to be true.

Action generators and sense-making

ALCO knew about Leeson's escalating margin calls, market rumour, instructions defied and so forth. Why did it not see those indicators for what they were? To reframe the question, what sustained the ruling myth of a star trader successfully exploiting a bubble of profit?

Evidence suggests that once a myth gains credence, considerable challenge and disconfirmation may be needed to demolish it as established structures, patterns of data collection, analysis and other organizational activities becomes associated with it (e.g. Drummond 1998b, Kuhn 1970; Ross and Staw 1993; Starbuck 1983). Meanwhile the organization risks being pulled off course as these action generators tend to exclude from the decision-making arena information that is inconsistent with the ruling myth.

ALCO saw what they expected to see, namely a cash hungry business. Ron Baker said:

> What you would definitely expect to see in a situation where you are making a lot of money from a low risk arbitrage is a lot of capital employed to support the business . . . To me the fact that we had a large amount of capital out on the exchanges was one of the reasons why we felt comfortable about the level of profitability . . . because that was the way you were making the profit, through your ability to post large volumes of margins.
>
> (Evidence given to Treasury Committee, 23 July 1996)

Recall that action generators allow organizations to act unreflectively. Consequently when Hawes reports that Barings technically breached its daylight overdraft facility with Citibank, ALCO engages in so-called 'first order thinking', addressing the problem as Hawes defines it, never considering the possibility of 'a problem behind the problem' (e.g. Watzlawick et al. 1974).

It is unclear how ALCO 'knew' that Leeson's positions were matched – though information probably came from Leeson. What is clear is that ALCO never reflected on whether that 'fundamental premise' was in fact true. Instead ALCO rationalized market rumour to fit expectations by assuming that the market was reacting to partial information. If *all* risks had been monitored daily, as Barings claimed, the bank would not have collapsed. ALCO believed it was monitoring risk but ended up focusing on the wrong risks.

Recall that acting unreflectively usually means acting in a self-serving manner (Starbuck 1983). Even if Leeson's trades had been matched, it was dangerous to assume that there was no risk attached. In order to make sense of their environments, decision-makers need to create terms for complex phenomena (e.g. March 1981). The term 'matched positions' masked the time lag between buying and selling as positions are never *exactly* matched in arbitrage. Moreover, there is always the possibility that another trader may be doing the same thing. While the risk is slight where only a few contracts are being traded, ALCO ignored the much bigger risk implied by arbitraging thousands of contracts – ultimately half the entire futures market.

Yet the very fact that in 1994 Baker had seen fit to impose limits on Leeson's trading was a tacit acknowledgement of risk. Waltz too was becoming worried that there were no effective limits in place. In the language of phenomenological sociology, ALCO used the term 'matched positions' to abolish risk rather like organizations use notions of strategic planning to abolish the unpredictable future (Brown 1978, 1989; see also Drummond 2001). Consequently the very real risk inherent in Leeson's alleged trading was not officially recognized and therefore ignored.

Self-enhancement

'They wanted to believe it was all true,' says Leeson (1996: 217). Leeson's comment implies that his apparent success enhanced colleagues' self-esteem – even those who did not profit directly such as settlements staff in London. Such behaviour is consistent with theories of self-enhancement that suggest we perceive or construe ambiguous or equivocal information in a manner that suits our purpose (e.g. Pfeffer and Fong 2005). 'Huge liquidity and gaps,' says Sacranie. It sounds good when in fact Sacranie is merely recycling nonsense in currency. Gueler dismisses Leeson's mystery customer as 'insane', though he does not doubt that Barings has been clever enough to profit from his alleged insanity – so clever in fact that Barings is straining credibility. Baker too states that competitors covet Barings' success.

Self-enhancement may also have dissuaded actors from asking questions for fear of looking foolish. Escalation theory predicts that the longer actors professed to believe in Leeson's phenomenal profits, norms for consistency are likely to make it increasingly difficult to question that belief. One way of sustaining a self-serving belief is to avoid situations or information that might contradict it. Waltz realizes that many of Leeson's explanations are nonsense but limits the amount of interrogation she engages in. It is doubtful whether anyone in Barings properly understood the complicated rules surrounding margin calls. Yet no one admitted it. When Ron Baker is asked to explain why Leeson is making so much money, he can only say, 'I trust the guy a fair bit' – in other words, 'I do not know'.

Leeson realized that product managers regarded it as demeaning to involve themselves in detail. Consequently they failed to notice the inconsistencies in his numbers and Baker gave Kelly incorrect information about the arrangements for collecting margin from customers.

The missing hero

Leeson exploited his conference with Norris to reassure other actors about what he was doing. The precise effects are unclear but they may well have been to relieve individuals of perceived responsibility to act. They can justify their non-intervention to themselves on the grounds that Peter Norris is apparently fully briefed on Leeson's trading, just as bystanders in the rape scene assumed some-one else would call the police (e.g. Platt 1973).

Herding behaviour may also have helped to sustain the myth. Herding theory predicts that in order to save time and effort, actors base their decisions on 'safety in numbers'. For example, prospective customers sometimes base their choice of restaurant on the number of people already eating there. They assume that the food must be good when in fact all that may have happened is that people have followed one another like sheep. For example, if someone in Barings had taken the trouble to obtain statements directly from Osaka and SIMEX and compared them, they would immediately have discovered that Leeson's positions were completely open. Herding may explain why no one bothered to check this pivotal assumption. Leeson's positions must be matched because everyone said so.

The politics of escalation

The alleged SLK transaction is the most important incident in the whole story because even if Leeson's explanation had been true, he had committed a sackable offence and should have been suspended immediately pending an inquiry. Indeed Peter Norris subsequently had the grace to acknowledge that he regarded his handling of the incident as his most culpable failure (Treasury Committee, 10 June 1996).

The failure was by no means Norris's alone. Barley and Tolbert (1997; see also Rudolph and Repenning 2002) suggest that for institutions like apartheid and communism to tumble, what is needed is for disparate actors to start moving in the same direction. This book suggests that organizations are vulnerable to a similar dynamic. In a nutshell the 'SLK transaction' prompted key actors to 'move with', that is, protect Leeson, in the process destroying vital organizational checks and balances.

Managers perpetually occupied with controlling opportunism are by definition distracted from the main task of the business (Ghoshal and Moran 1996, citing Barnard 1938). On the other hand, since investment banking can involve potentially catastrophic risks, it is imperative that investment banks strike a balance between the pursuit of profit and a disciplined approach to risk. Striking a balance involves give and take:

> The advantage of organizations . . . [lies] in leveraging ability to take initiative, to cooperate and learn . . . Organizations fail when they are unable to build trust and commitment.
>
> (Ghosal and Moran 1996: 42)

This quotation could almost be an epitaph for Barings. Instead of leveraging initiative, cooperation and learning necessary to assemble the various pieces of the jigsaw pointing to malfeasance, Leeson's managers latterly destroyed it by allowing fear and interpersonal tensions to sway their judgement.

Greed first: real power in organizations is frequently unobtrusive as it resides in so-called 'non-decisions', that is, the taken-for-granted assumptions about what is appropriate (e.g. Bachrach and Baratz 1963). Non-decisions are evidenced by 'what is not' in the organization – including that which never appears on the agenda. The correct course of action in response to Leeson's escalating margin calls and poor accounting would have been for ALCO to have done what it claimed to do, namely engage in active management of risk by suspending Leeson's trading pending proper reconciliation. Significantly, the possibility was never even mentioned. Moreover, when Hopkins takes the initiative by attempting to highlight Barings' poor systems of control and to specify the correct state of affairs, he receives short shrift. Replacing him with Baker on the Management Committee signifies where Barings' real priorities lie. Moreover, even the items pertaining to risk that do reach the agenda are not taken seriously. ALCO never even asks why Leeson's positions have increased, far less takes any effective action to ensure its instructions are complied with.

There was panic as well as greed. If prison warders report too many misdemeanours by inmates, they risk having their own competence called into question. Inmates exploit this paradox to commit rule infringements. By the same token the discovery of the alleged 'SLK transaction' called into question the conduct of Bax, Jones and Baker, and to a lesser extent Norris. They had a vested interest, therefore, in playing down the issue by describing it as an 'operational error' and a 'back office glitch' instead of an act of gross misconduct. If Baker had asked to see the paperwork for the transaction, he would have realized that his signature had been forged. He was more interested in preventing 'time consuming' questions and ensuring no 'gigantic investigation' or into this 'pretty sound' business.

As systems of cooperation, organizations realize their power through relationships which enable actors to coordinate their efforts (e.g. Ghoshal and Moran 1996; Knights and Roberts 1982). The breakdown of relations between key actors, and Leeson's adroit exploitation of the resultant interpersonal tensions, undermined the power of organization because it impeded sensemaking – thus perpetuating a state of ignorance about the real nature of Leeson's trading. Political tensions also precluded Jones from conferring with Broadhurst and other key actors in London. For instance, Jones could ill afford to get deeply into discussions with colleagues about whether the alleged SLK transaction had been funded by excess margin, because it would have shown that he had not been supervising Leeson – contrary to his instructions. Railton too is instructed by Gamby not to probe. Then there is the bizarre instruction to Granger *not* to contact SLK for confirmation of the alleged transaction– the most obvious step of all.

Hawes's attempts to investigate the alleged SLK transaction are blocked by Baker. Baker is supported by Bax and Jones, who are equally anxious to extricate Leeson from the 'loop'. Recall that Becker (1960) suggested that entrapment can result through the making of side-bets, namely extraneous investments that gradually accumulate, thereby making it hard for decision-makers to change direction. By identifying with Leeson's profits, Baker has entered into side-bets by making himself responsible for Leeson. Baker's ill-disguised irritation with Hawes may have sprung from being confronted with undeniable evidence that Hawes knew significantly more about the 'SLK transaction' than he did (Secretary of State versus Baker). Baker's 'ballistic' response to Hawes's questions undermines one of the most important organizational checks and balances:

Authority cannot be imposed or individually possessed, but always remains only a quality of the relationship *between* people, in which *both* are personally committed to, and see as legitimate the reciprocal rights and obligations realized through their interaction.

(Knights and Roberts 1982: 50, italics in original)

When Baker puts his instrumental concerns for profit and self-enhancement above cooperating with Hawes's legitimate enquiries, the quality of the relation is destroyed (Giddens 1979; Knights and Roberts 1982). Authority failed in Barings because there was no adequate acknowledgement by traders and those who managed them of their dependence upon financial controllers to insist upon a disciplined approach to risk-taking. Consequently at a crucial point in the organization's history, Barings is governed by relations of raw power rather than authority. You could almost call it anarchy.

Recall that escalation tends to be more pronounced where decisions to reinvest can be made passively. Meanwhile in the midst of near anarchy, margin calls for millions of pounds are automatically triggered by SIMEX and paid almost automatically. It is the relentless but in many ways invisible flow of funds out of London that bankrupts Barings.

13   The illusion of control

Life is a gamble, at terrible odds – if it was a bet you wouldn't take it.
(*Rosencrantz and Guildenstern are Dead*, Stoppard 1967: 86)

Barings never forgot the terrible lessons of 1890. The bank maintained its decidedly risk-averse policy and yet paradoxically ended up incurring catastrophic exposure to risk. Theoretically we would have expected the complete opposite to have happened. That is, Barings would have been more likely to have missed opportunities for expansion, development and profit generation through being too cautious.

Consider the cliché that entrepreneurs don't take risks; they do things that other people think are risky. This statement implies that two people can see the same opportunity and arrive at a different evaluation of the risk involved. By risk is meant the 'extent to which there is uncertainty about whether potentially significant or disappointing outcomes of decisions will be realized' (Sitkin and Pablo 1992: 9). Sitkin and Pablo's definition of risk involves three dimensions. These are:

- outcome uncertainty
- outcome expectations
- outcome potential.

We can thus define decisions as riskier to the extent that:

- expected outcomes are more uncertain
- decision goals are difficult to achieve
- a potential outcome set involves some extreme consequences.

Risk perception refers to the decision-maker's subjective appraisal of these three dimensions of risk. The argument is that since there is no certainty about any of them, the decision-makers assessment of risk is bound to be subjective to some extent. Subjectivity creates scope for misjudgement, over or under optimism.

According to Sitkin and Pablo (1992) decision-makers with high risk-taking propensity tend to perceive less risk than objective analysis would suggest.

Consequently a decision-maker with high risk-taking propensity will attend to and weigh positive outcomes more highly and thus will tend to overestimate the probability of gain relative to the probability of loss. A decision-maker with low risk-taking propensity is likely to err in the opposite direction. In other words they will attend to and weigh negative outcomes more highly and thus will tend to underestimate the probability of gain relative to the probability of loss. A risk-averse decision-maker will thus perceive choices as involving higher risk than objective analysis would suggest appropriate (see also Forlani and Mullins 2000). In other words, whereas a gung-ho decision-maker is likely to take a cavalier attitude to risk, a risk-averse individual is likely to be too cautious where they could and should take a risk.

There is another reason for expecting Barings to have been unduly risk averse. Prospect theory predicts that when decision-makers perceive themselves as being faced with a choice between gains, they typically prefer a definite gain to one that is merely probable even though the latter has a higher monetary value. For instance, the theory predicts that a definite gain of £100 is likely to be preferable to a 50 per cent chance of winning £200 or nothing at all. Prospect theory thus implies that organizations like Barings who are in favourable circumstances are more likely to be risk averse than risk seeking because they feel that by involving themselves in uncertain enterprises they may risk losing everything (Kahneman and Tversky 1979; see also Whyte 1986, 1991b).

Given that it is axiomatic in investment banking that higher profits entail higher risk, we would have expected Barings' Management Committee to have been alarmed about Leeson's escalating profits. It is a matter of record that collectively no particular anxiety was expressed. As we shall see, the members of the Management Committee believed that they were behaving prudently in supporting Leeson's trading. I intend to suggest that this misjudgement reflected an illusion of invulnerability.

The illusion of invulnerability

In 1923 Frederick Banting and John Macleod won the Nobel Prize for the discovery of insulin. Banting claimed that Macleod had been more of a hindrance than a help, while Macleod omitted Banting's name from all the speeches describing the research leading up to the discovery. In a fascinating book Susan Taylor (1980) suggests that this is typical human behaviour, that we all possess an over-inflated view of our own capabilities while tending to denigrate the accomplishments of others in a perpetual drive for self-enhancement. For example, says Taylor, consider the daily 'to do' list. Few of us ever get anywhere near accomplishing all the tasks that we set ourselves, but it rarely stops us from making up a new list each day. In Taylor's view, incidentally, depression results not from seeing things as worse than they are, but as they are!

To be more precise, self-enhancement refers to 'the desire or observed reality of seeing oneself and by extension one's actions, traits, and attitudes in the most positive light' (Pfeffer and Fong 2005: 374). In other words, as human beings we possess an innate tendency to perceive ourselves as superior to other people, to see ourselves more positively than others see us, and to believe ourselves to be above average.

Such beliefs can have important ramifications for decision-making. We are likely to overestimate the impact of our own contributions to the success of an enterprise while underestimating the impact of contributions made by other people. We are willing to take credit for success but frequently derogate the accomplishments of other people, particularly if we see ourselves as in competition with them.

Our innate desire for self-enhancement can produce suboptimal decisions. Staw and Hoang (1995) found that team managers tended to field players that they had paid a lot of money to acquire more frequently than their less expensive acquisitions, regardless of their actual goal-scoring record. Obviously star players tend to attract crowds but such behaviour may also be driven ego-defensiveness as managers unconsciously say to themselves, 'I chose him, therefore he must be good.'

Certainly evidence suggests that ego-involvement in a decision biases our perceptions. Schoorman (1988) found that supervisors who were personally responsible for selecting new employees subsequently gave those employees better performance ratings than they gave to staff they did not personally select. Conversely supervisors who disagreed with a decision to hire someone subsequently gave that employee a lower rating than their performance actually merited (Bazerman et al. 1982). In 2006 Cadbury's was forced to withdraw millions of bars of confectionary following a salmonella scare. Cadbury's had known about potential contamination for months but argued that the risk was insignificant. They also revised their 'in-house' criterion about what constituted 'safe' levels of contamination. While Cadbury's may have been risk seeking, that is unwilling to incur a definite loss, another plausible possibility is that the decision-makers simply could not believe that *their* product was unwholesome.

Our innate desire as human beings for self-enhancement can manifest itself in an oblique fashion. Festinger's (1957) dissonance theory posited that any two cognitive elements (any knowledge, opinion or belief about oneself or the environment) which are inconsistent with one another will lead to psychological disturbance. We tend to cope with such disturbance by rationalizing the situation to eliminate the dissonance. In a fascinating experiment, supermarket customers were allowed to choose between obtaining scouring pads on a trial basis or as a final purchase. Those who opted to make a final purchase subsequently reported that they liked the brand more than customers who took the pads on a trial basis (cited in Salancik 1977).

Illusion heightened

Illusion of control and invulnerability extend to believing that we can control events that are entirely due to chance. For example, what would you prefer, to choose your own lottery ticket or to accept a ticket handed to you by the shopkeeper? (You can assume the shopkeeper is honest). Logically it makes no difference to the probability of winning either way, but a good many people would prefer to choose their own ticket as if they can somehow influence the outcome. Likewise, research into gambling behaviour has shown that players typically shake the cup softly when needing a low number on the dice while giving it a good rattle if requiring a high number (Langer 1983; see also Griffiths 1990; Whyte et al. 1997)!

Life may be a game at hopeless odds but if you are allowed to deal the cards you might just take the bet. This is because being in control makes us feel we can influence outcomes and we are therefore willing to take a bigger risk than we otherwise might. For instance, research into gambling behaviour shows that players tend to bet more if they can deal the cards (Langer 1983). The illusion of control is likely to be heightened when the game involves skill as well as chance. This is why fruit machines incorporate 'nudge' and 'hold' buttons. The aim is to encourage players to feed coins into the machine by imparting an illusory sense of control whereby players judge they can influence the outcome of the game by judicious selection of buttons.

Impact of repeated success

Paradoxically it may be the most successful organizations that are most prone to decision error resulting from the illusion of control. Although the proverb teaches that nothing succeeds like success, success tends to breed overconfidence because it confirms our competence. When we feel competent, we may take bigger risks than objective conditions appear to warrant because our success persuades us that we cannot fail. For example, research into gambling behaviour shows that early wins in games of chance encourage players to bet more (Langer 1983).

This point was graphically demonstrated on 28 January 1986 when a television audience of millions saw the spaceship *Challenger* lift off and then immediately disintegrate into a ball of flame, killing everyone on board. The disaster happened because NASA had the experience of twenty-four successful launches working against them whereby shuttle launches had become regarded as routine events involving operational technology. Repeated success had changed NASA's attitude towards risk:

> When the shuttle flights continued to depart and return successfully, the criterion for a launch – convince me that I should send *Challenger* – was dropped. Underestimating the dynamic nature of reliability, managers inserted a new criterion – convince me that I shouldn't send Challenger.
>
> (Starbuck and Millken 1988: 331)

NASA's chief engineer Milton Silveria said:

> In the early days of the space program we were so damned uncertain that we always got everybody's opinion. We would ask for continual reviews, continual scrutiny . . . to look at this thing and make sure we were doing it right.

As we started to fly the shuttle again, (and again) I think the system developed a false confidence in itself.

(Starbuck and Milliken 1988: 331)

Seigmund Warburg said that the worst thing that could happen to the upstart bank he founded was that it should become part of the City establishment. In Warburg's view establishment status implied a temptation to become lazy, self-satisfied and complacent (Reich 1980). That is precisely what did happen after Warburg retired from the bank. His successors abandoned their relatively cheap and modest premises for much more lavish surroundings and began a hugely ambitious programme of diversification, including acquiring the public school firm of stockbrokers Rowe and Pitman, thereby diluting Warburg's meritocracy. The last straw was an ill-advised incursion into the United States that cost the now bloated firm its independence: 'Such was Warburg's sky-high reputation – an estimate fully shared by Warburg's itself – that no one could have imagined how rapidly the wheels would fall off' (Kynaston 2001: 759).

Deadly shortcuts

The manner in which decision-makers process information can sustain the illusion of control. In order to gain a grasp of complex problems, decision-makers must simplify them. They do this by the application of heuristics, mental short-cuts in other words. The trouble is that some of the shortcuts taken by decision-makers can lead to oversimplification whereby crucial data becomes omitted from the decision-maker's frame of reference (comprehensively reviewed in Bazerman 2001).

A heuristic of particular relevance to this book is the so-called 'representativeness' bias – or reasoning by analogy (Kahneman and Tversky 1972). Reasoning by analogy saves cognitive effort as decision-makers judge a present case by its resemblance to the past. Doctors constantly use this shortcut when diagnosing illnesses. For instance every case of influenza is different but all cases exhibit certain general features that are amenable to rapid classification and similar treatment. Speeding up decision-making in this way involves a risk as doctors who see only what they expect to see may exclude the signs of a more serious ailment from their diagnosis.

Another word for reasoning by analogy is stereotyping. Stereotyping can happen unconsciously. For instance, evidence suggests that even individuals with no explicit hostile attitude towards women or ethnic minority groups may nevertheless still hold implicit associations consistent with common stereotypes, and those implicit attitudes can influence what individuals see and how they see (Banaji and Greenwald 1995). The US military's stereotyped view of the Vietcong as primitive peasants blinded them to the enemy's growing military sophistication and caused the US military to seriously underestimate the enemy's capacity to resist (Janis 1989).

Wilson et al. (1996) studied a brewery that succumbed to reasoning by analogy. The brewery employed just thirty-five people and produced beer in small quantity.

Demand for good quality beer was growing and the firm's management were considering how best to exploit the possibilities when they were offered the chance to acquire a redundant brewery. The putative acquisition seemed like a tremendous opportunity because it offered an eightfold increase in capacity for much less money than the other option of doubling on-site capacity. They decided to take the opportunity even though a non-executive director resigned over the decision to proceed.

The non-executive director's reservations were well founded. The boiler and lifting gear proved unreliable and the effluent treatment plant became inadequate when the government introduced tighter laws. More importantly the inflows of revenues in large-scale production were slower and margins thinner than the management were used to with a smaller, more tightly controlled operation. The result was a cash flow crisis followed by a forced merger. The company overbalanced in reaching for such a large volume when it might have sustained a lesser increase. A decision-maker said afterwards:

> Really, we seized an opportunity rather than made a planned decision . . . we felt we could hardly turn it [the purchase of the brewery] down. We were planning to spend £150,000 expanding our own brewery and the acquisition only cost £115,000.
>
> (Wilson et al. 1996: 1003)

The brewery managers thought they were making a good decision based on their knowledge of the industry. The venture failed because they ignored important differences between the two operations. The decision is also an example of the kind of myopia that can develop when decision-makers are presented with an opportunity that seems too good to lose and they seize it without properly considering the possible negative aspects of the venture (Janis 1989).

Group dynamics

Decisions in complex organizations are frequently made in groups. Groups can make better decisions than individuals as they enable information sharing and dialogue between people with different expertise and mind sets. Cohesive groups can also provide a measure of psychological security in testing times when, for example, the group is facing a hostile environment. Cohesion also contributes to individual's self-esteem (Janis 1982).

There may be a price to be paid, however. Since responsibility within groups is shared, groups may not always exercise appropriate rigour when it comes to decision-making and may exhibit and even amplify individual biases for escalation and risk-seeking behaviour.

Such biases include a possible tendency for groups to take a more risk or a more cautious decision than an individual decision-maker would take. Polarization is another form of bias. Polarization refers to situations where the post-discussion response is more extreme in the same direction as the average of pre-discussion responses. In other words, polarization thesis assumes that members begin group discussion having already formed a view of the issues and group discussions tend to magnify individual preferences which can lead to a more extreme response than an individual would make.

Group decision-making can also be undermined by norms and status differences whereby members deliberately refrain from expressing their view for fear of contravening protocol or contradicting more powerful others (e.g. Kerr and Tindale 2003; Shaw 1981; Zander 1982). Norms, in particular, can exert a powerful hold over behaviour because conformity to norms is the basic price to be paid for group membership. Norms are collective behavioural expectations (e.g. Habermas 1988, 1992) over issues that are important to the group. Examples of group norms include an unspoken requirement to dress in a certain way, to avoid using bad language and to refrain from speaking until spoken to. Breaking norms means inviting censure from others when important obligations and expectations are not met (Goffman 1967). Group members conform to norms to protect themselves from those social penalties. The risk however is that they become habituated to conducting themselves within the confines of a normative web.

Logically you might think that the more cohesive the group is, the stronger it will become. In fact cohesion is potentially double edged as cohesive groups may experience a reduction in decision-making capability due to a phenomenon known as groupthink. Groupthink is characterized by a reduction in analytical rigour as members of the group stop challenging one another for fear of upsetting the cosy atmosphere. Consequently the discussion becomes confined to only a few alternatives; the group loses sight of what it is trying to achieve and the values implicated by choice. There is no re-examination of risks of initially preferred choice of action or any effective attempt to re-examine courses of action initially rejected. Expert evaluations are dispensed with and the group is also likely to ignore or downplay feedback inconsistent with their preferred viewpoint. Moreover the group is likely to skip contingency planning, for example, how decisions might be hindered by bureaucratic inertia, chance events and so forth. The group is also likely to be convinced of the morality of its own actions even though those actions may be morally questionable.

Groupthink results in self-censorship as members unconsciously suppress their doubts thus creating the illusion that the group is unanimous. When a group who respect one another's opinions then reach an apparently unanimous view, each member tends to feel the belief must be true; reliance on consensual validation thus replaces individual critical thinking. Moreover, by supporting one another group members tend to play up areas of convergence at the expense of exploring divergences. Since there is no reality testing the result is an illusion of invulnerability.

Janis (1982) cites Pearl Harbor in 1941 and the Bay of Pigs fiasco in 1961 as archetypal cases of large-scale decision debacles caused by groupthink. Pearl Harbor happened because of a failure to boost the defences of the United States' largest naval base despite warnings that an attack might be imminent. For example, shortly before the attack the American military learned that employees of the Japanese consulate in Hawaii were burning papers but the implications of this development were ignored as the American military unanimously agreed that Pearl Harbor was impregnable. Although intelligence indicated that Japan was preparing a massive attack, reports did not indicate where it would fall. Such ambiguity, says Janis, left room for collective misjudgements based on wishful thinking. Wishful thinking then resulted in military commanders paying attention to signals consistent with their expectations, that an attack was imminent elsewhere. Moreover their stereotyped view of Japanese impotence failed to recognize that things had changed. The US blockade was depriving Japan of essential supplies of oil, cotton and other raw materials, creating a desperate situation likely to provoke an equally desperate response.

Since military commanders agreed that the target could not possibly be Pearl Harbor, there was no alert until the bombs began exploding at eight o'clock on a Sunday morning when many personnel were on weekend leave or just getting up. Moreover, because of the low state of alert there was no air reconnaissance and therefore no chance of spotting the planes on approach. The result of the denouement that Sunday morning was 2000 personnel killed outright, and as many again injured or missing in the worst naval or military disaster in American history. Interestingly some naval commanders refused to believe the reassuring messages emanating from senior command and drilled their ships' companies in emergency responses. The survival rate on those ships was significantly higher than on vessels that were completely unprepared.

In 1961 disaster struck again when the United States attempted to land a military force in Cuba without providing air cover. Air cover was seen as superfluous because Castro's army was perceived to be so weak that a small brigade would easily defeat it and the (obsolete) US B26 bombers would easily destroy Castro's ground forces. The only contingency plan was that in the unlikely event of the invasion failing to attain its objective, troops could retire to mountain caves. No one asked the military planners about the precise location of the caves. In fact troops were separated from shelter by eighty kilometres of jungle swamp. 'This oversight might have been corrected if someone in the advisory group had taken the trouble to look at a map of Cuba, available in any atlas' (Janis 1982: 27). Instead troops were dispatched to the killing ground without an escape route.

Janis (1982) suggests that in this case the illusion of invulnerability arose because Kennedy had been so successful in the run-up to the presidential elections since 1956 that with Kennedy leading them and with all the talent he had assembled, the group believed that they were unstoppable. Another factor was that Kennedy wanted to preserve the team spirit that he had built up. Then there was the emergence of a so-called 'mind-guard', namely the president's brother Robert Kennedy. When some members of the executive committee began to develop reservations about the plan, Robert Kennedy emphatically told them to keep quiet on the grounds that the president had made up his mind and that their role was now to support the decision to invade.

14 The last line of defence

The sun was shining on the sea,
Shining with all his might;
. . . And this was odd, because it was
The middle of the night.

(Lewis Carroll, *Through the Looking Glass*)

Amazing recovery

We come now to the final phase of the story as we focus upon the strategic apex of the organization and what the Management Committee that met weekly on Mondays saw. The story begins in September 1993 when Peter Baring attended a meeting at the Bank of England. It was a routine event, one of the mechanisms used by the Bank in discharging its regulatory role in overseeing the safety and integrity of the banking system as a whole. Earlier the Bank of England had been concerned when Barings had been obliged to discreetly borrow $75 million to support operations after Barings Securities made an £80 million loss. By September 1993, it seemed as though the worst was over. The minutes of the meeting record that Peter Baring said, '"The recovery in profitability has been amazing," leaving Barings to conclude that it was not actually very difficult to make money in the securities business' (Treasury Committee, 15 May 1996: 22).

After the bank collapsed, Peter Baring was asked to explain what he meant by this statement. Baring replied:

> Contrary to Christopher Heath and some of his colleagues who believed that the future of agency broking in foreign markets was limited, that we believed it had a distinct and positive future. Our then current experience was show-ing that to be the case.
>
> (Evidence given to Treasury Committee, 15 May 1996: 22)

Moreover, by now initiatives were well in hand to bring Barings Securities firmly under control. The aim was to combine all of the investment banking businesses of Barings into a single business unit in a single location. Barings' deputy chairman and second most senior figure, Andrew Tuckey, said:

> This concept was developed because of a difficult relationship . . . between the centre of Barings and the people who were running Baring Securities . . . The ethos was really, that the last thing you need in a stock-broking outfit is management in a formal bureaucratic sense. Everything in the broker's world is today and tomorrow . . . whereas when you talk to a corporate finance person he is interested in what his clients are going to be doing next year.
>
> (Secretary of State versus Tuckey)

An important consequence of combining organizations was that the financial accounts were also combined to reflect a single organization. Solo consolidation as it became known meant that from late 1993, Baring Brothers and Barings Securities London were treated as one unit for capital purposes in the UK. Consequently Baring Brothers could move as much money as they liked to Singapore to meet Leeson's margin calls:

> The principle of solo consolidation is that the bridge between Baring Brothers and Baring Securities was taken away and the two were pushed together, so that any amount of cash that was agreed could go from Baring Brothers into Baring Securities . . . Our money market people were told they could fund Baring Securities without limitation. Then we designed various constraints to go round that which . . . the accounting system of Baring Securities completely defeated.
>
> (Evidence given by George Maclean, Head of Banking, in Secretary of State versus Tuckey)

'Buried reasonably deep ...'

Such freedom was subject to one important legal constraint known as the 'large exposures' rule, whereby banks are forbidden to lend more than 25 per cent of their capital to any one client. The rule is intended to protect investors by preventing banks from becoming overly exposed to a single client should that client default. In May 1994 Barings was posting so much money to SIMEX that it decided it had better check with Christopher Thompson at the Bank of England whether the rule applied to margin payments posted as short term 'loans to clients'. Thompson promised to investigate. No more was heard until 6 September 1994 when Barings' Head of Banking, George Maclean, telephoned Thompson to report that Barings had now breached that limit. Maclean now needed to know where Barings stood legally:

> Thompson said he was aware that he owed us a response but that the matter was buried reasonably deep in his in-tray. He said, however, that he was

relaxed about the exposure on the basis of our view that the exposure was in effect to all members of the Exchange . . . He was happy with us having reported the situation and that we should continue to exceed 25% of our capital base from time to time.

(Evidence given by George Maclean to Board of Banking
Supervision 1995: 173)

The Bank of England has no record of this conversation but in any case in February 1995 the informal concession was withdrawn. Even then Barings was given time and some flexibility to adjust to the rules – a reflection of the Bank of England's regard for Barings:

The Bank regarded the controls in Barings as informal but effective. It had confidence in Barings' senior management, many of whom were long standing Barings' employees. Accordingly, it placed greater reliance on statements made to it by management than it would have done had this degree of confidence not existed.

(Board of Banking Supervision 1995: 244)

Compliance with this new rule was an issue that would exercise Barings' senior managers during the last days of the bank's existence. How could they meet escalating demands for margin yet remain within the law? MANCO discussed the problem on 6 February. No one knew, and nor did anyone enquire how large the exposure was. Mr Tuckey subsequently said he would have been 'surprised' had he known the amount involved was £500 million (Secretary of State versus Tuckey).

MANCO was also aware that in April 1994 a Wall Street trader named Joseph Jett had been sacked by his employers Kidder Peabody when it was discovered that he had been declaring false profits of $350 million. In the wake of the ensuing scandal, MANCO ordered a review of internal controls and had learned that there were weaknesses, because controllers in London were unable to monitor overseas offices properly. By early 1995 MANCO understood that the requisite system was 'in the process of being developed' (Fay 1996: 131). The following week, 13 February, the need for such a system was again highlighted when MANCO learned about the SLK transaction. The report was presented in a low key fashion as a settlements error and was received without comment. 'We had become familiar with settlement problems,' said Andrew Tuckey (Secretary of State versus Tuckey).

Defying gravity

In early 1994 Peter Norris had something embarrassing to report to the Management Committee. Nick Leeson had been arrested for indecent exposure. Although the charge was subsequently reduced to a misdemeanour, it was still serious misconduct by someone acting as the bank's ambassador. This was the first time MANCO had heard of Leeson. It might have been the last time too as they considered sacking him. They were dissuaded by Norris, who explained that Leeson was a central figure in the 'amazing recovery' of the securities business.

It was a decision that appeared to be vindicated as Leeson's reported revenues for the first half of 1994 were about £12 million. In November Ron Baker submitted a note to the Management Committee on the performance of his Special Products Group during 1994: 'It has been a great year for volatility trading until the final quarter. Even then our JGB SIMEX trading had benefited from volatility being crushed' (Secretary of State versus Tuckey).

It may have been a great year but there was a shadow over the future and whether Leeson's profits would last. Peter Baring said:

> We had a number of businesses that were low risk and relatively high profitability; the most pronounced example of this was the Japanese warrant trading business . . . We had a number of businesses of that order of magnitude . . . [that] were low risk and high profitability. What none of us believed was that this business would last. The basic instinct behind the BoBS's [Board of Banking Supervision] comment that there is something about this business that defied gravity is something which we shared; but it was in terms of its durability . . . In our experience, these businesses could last for a period but then they would go. That would happen to us again and again.
>
> (Treasury Committee, 15 May1996: 22)

Other members of MANCO agreed with Peter Baring's judgement. For example, the minutes of a meeting in November 1994 record: 'We have to expect our arbitrage business between Tokyo, Osaka and Singapore will decline in the face of stronger competition' (Secretary of State versus Tuckey). Another issue discussed by the Management Committee was whether 'other opportunities could be developed using similar concepts elsewhere' (Secretary of State versus Tuckey). In other words, could Barings keep ahead of the competition by seeking new markets in which to practise Leeson's style of arbitrage?

'We certainly couldn't expect it to last ...'

At every meeting MANCO received the following information:

- monthly management accounts
- group weekly income reports
- Barings Investment Bank daily income reports
- summaries of the Group Weekly Income reports
- weekly divisional reports.

The members of the committee could therefore, if they chose, monitor developments day by day, while not losing sight of the larger picture afforded by weekly and monthly data. In practice, despite moves to merge organizations to create a more modern integrated bank, the partnership culture still prevailed in Barings. Each director usually gave a brief report on events in their division. It would be unusual for members to question one another and unthinkable for there to be any open expression of conflict. Contestable issues would be dealt with outside the meeting.

Leeson's profits became particularly noticeable to the committee towards the end of January 1995 in the wake of the earthquake in Japan, including the massive reported revenues for January 24 – almost £1 million in a single day. MANCO was given to understand that the sudden upsurge in profitability resulted from unusual market conditions that Barings had been clever enough to exploit. MANCO was also aware of the strain on funding and the disquiet in the market. ALCO's recommendation temporarily curtailing Leeson's trading was approved without demur.

One of MANCO's duties was to notice and act upon anything unusual. On Monday 6 February 1995 Peter Norris made a special verbal report highlighting Leeson's £3.2 million ($9 million) profit for the previous week. Diarmid Kelly was sceptical: 'You do not make $9 million in a week with no risk,' he said (Gapper and Denton 1996: 291). Norris then reiterated the by now familiar explanation of Leeson's trading. That too was accepted without detailed questioning. Andrew Tuckey said: 'Increased volatility did not mean increased risk because we were told and we believed that the positions were fully matched (subject to the small intra-day limits)' (Secretary of State versus Tuckey, italics removed). Leeson's reported revenues for January 1995 outstripped those of Barings Investment Bank by about 133 per cent. Yet the Management Committee never asked whether Leeson might be breaking his small intra-day limits.

Tuckey accepted ALCO's description of Leeson's trading as a business 'conducted essentially without risk' (Secretary of State versus Tuckey). What did 'essentially without risk' mean, especially given that it had been thought necessary to impose limits? Tuckey again:

> I did not think there was any risk in it. I knew there was some risk, and the risk I understood is there is no price risk because they were equal and opposite transactions. There was a very small risk of time in that by the time you sell and by the time you buy there is a minute or so when you might not be able to complete the trade. There was no authority . . . to carry the position overnight, so that position had to be closed, so the only residual risk was a counterparty risk.
>
> (Secretary of State versus Tuckey)

Tuckey too believed the bubble must eventually burst:

> So there was familiarity in Barings with the fact that a business like this could arise and given our position we could take advantage of it, but we certainly couldn't expect it to last.
>
> (Secretary of State versus Tuckey)

Business as usual

The Management Committee met for the last time on 20 February 1995. Unlike Peter Norris, who could concentrate full-time on management, Andrew Tuckey had client responsibilities. At that time he was involved in advising a large takeover bid, an activity that absorbed much of his time. Tuckey said:

> In an investment bank or merchant bank the person who brings in the business is the person who commands a great deal of respect in the organization. That leadership role is different from management as such . . . That is what people looked to me to do . . . Much of my working day was spent in helping people win business and also in doing the business myself.
>
> (Secretary of State versus Tuckey)

Even so, legally Andrew Tuckey was responsible for ensuring that matters coming before MANCO were properly considered. The committee now learned that Schroeder's had contacted Barings to warn them of rumours that Barings was overexposed on SIMEX due to problems with a counterparty and that, far from being reduced, Leeson's gross position now stood at $3.1 billion.

MANCO was unperturbed by this information. There was little discussion of either issue. There was alarm, however, of sorts. Peter Baring said: 'When I finally saw the January 1995 figures, which I saw a number of days before the crisis broke, those figures seemed to me alarming in . . . that I believed this could not last' (Treasury Committee, 15 May 1996: 21).

Although 1993 had been a good year for investment banks, the volatile trading conditions of 1994 had proved damaging for many. Barings was apparently an exception. On Wednesday 24 February 1995 the directors met to consider the financial results for the whole group. Pre-tax profits were up from £100 million in 1993 to £102 million. Leeson apparently made £12.7 million as against £8.486 million for the remainder of Barings Investment Bank. The minutes of that meeting state:

> Profits were substantially assisted by a very high level of arbitrage income on the JGB and Nikkei indices. The level of this business will have to be scaled back, at least partly because the form in which transactions are reported by exchanges is liable to generate adverse financial comment.
>
> (Summary of Evidence, Secretary of State versus certain
Barings' Directors)

The words 'substantially assisted' are a euphemism. Without Leeson's apparent profits, Barings Investment Bank would have been trading at a loss.

15 Analysing the illusion of control

'It was the last thing I expected.'
(Evidence given by Peter Baring to Treasury Committee 1996: 29)

The focal question for analysis is how a risk-averse bank that, in theory, should have seen danger at every turn, not only ended up with catastrophic exposure to risk but also was oblivious to it. In an intriguing analysis of the psychodynamics of Barings' collapse, Stein (2000) argues that the anxiety associated with deregulation (Big Bang) drove Barings to seek as saviour an opposite or shadow to itself in terms of class and background – a role that Leeson would eventually fulfil.

Stein's thesis is that Barings sought an extreme risk-taker as opposite to its conservatism. Since the unconscious leaves no trace of itself, we can neither prove nor disprove the theory. What we can say is that it has resonance, for without Leeson's reported revenues Barings Investment Bank would have made a loss. Significantly, for all their grandeur, the members of MANCO decide that they cannot afford to sack Leeson for indecent exposure.

Mindful of Stein's thesis, how can other theories help to explain why MANCO failed to notice anything amiss? Recall that escalation tends to be worse where decisions to reinvest can be made passively as distinct from where they must be made actively (Brockner et al. 1979; Drummond 2004; Drummond and Chell 2002). When Barings first suggested moving to solo consolidation, the Bank of England demurred because it was conducive to malfeasance. It was a highly prescient comment as solo consolidation meant that one of the checks and balances in the system had been removed: there was now no limit on the amount of money that could be posted to Singapore.

The concession over the large exposures rule also facilitated passive reinvestment. The Bank of England's willingness to assist Barings raises an interesting issue. Historians of the City of London have highlighted the importance of social ties in gaining entry to business opportunities (e.g. Auger 2001; Kynaston 2001). Such exclusiveness was partly a reflection of the fact that a lot of business was conducted on the basis of trust. Trust refers to the expectation that another party would not act in self-interest at another's expense. For example, trust exists where

A knows that B will honour their obligations without the need for a written contract, hence the old motto of the stock exchange, 'my word is my bond'.

Trust is economically efficient because it saves time and can enable flexibility and therefore better resource allocation and adaptation. Personal ties also make expectations more predictable and reduce monitoring costs. In other words, trust does *not* operate like a calculated risk but as a heuristic. The heuristic element in this context is 'to assume the best when interpreting another's motives and actions. This heuristic quality is important because it speeds up decision making and conserves cognitive resources' (Uzzi 1999: 43).

Establishment status can benefit firms as research into the impact of social legitimacy shows that trusted firms are more likely to be granted loans and pay less interest than outsiders (Uzzi 1999). Had it been say a foreign bank, the Bank of England might have insisted upon the rules being applied – even if that bank had been well run. Yet it was willing to grant it to a multimillion pound organization run on informal lines because that organization was establishment and therefore trusted.

Yet as Warburg so astutely perceived, establishment status can become counterproductive, for example, if the network of organizations and institutions becomes overly entrenched and the conduct of business accordingly becomes overly cosy. This point was graphically and tragically demonstrated in the Paris air crash on Sunday 3 March 1974. A DC-10 operated by Turkish Airlines left Orly Airport at 12:30 pm bound for London. The plane was built by one of the best-run aerospace contractors in the United States. In addition, every aspect of the plane's design and construction had been approved by the Federal Aviation Administration. Unknown to the unfortunate 346 passengers on board, however, that particular DC-10 'had a lie in it'. Ten minutes after take-off 'the lie' caused the plane to crash, killing everyone on board.

According to McDonnell-Douglas, the company that built the plane and sold it to Turkish Airlines, the disaster was caused by an 'illiterate' baggage handler failing to close a cargo door properly. A *Sunday Times* investigation discovered, however, that although the handler Mahmoud Maham spoke no English, he had carried out his duties properly. Mahmoud Maham was not to know that the design of the DC-10's locking mechanism on its cargo doors was flawed in that they appeared locked when they were not.

As the *Sunday Times* investigation team delved further into the circumstances surrounding the crash, they discovered that a dress rehearsal had taken place two years earlier. In 1972 a cargo door blew off another DC-10 plane, sending a coffin plunging two miles to earth and leaving a flight attendant clinging desperately to remain inside the plane. When the door blew off, the sudden change in air pressure caused the cabin floor to collapse, severing vital cables. The crew, who had more experience of flying DC-10s than the Turkish Airlines pilot would have two years later, managed to land the plane safely. Even so, the incident clearly showed that the DC-10 required modifications to its cargo doors and vulnerable cabin floor.

According to the paperwork issued by McDonnell-Douglas, the requisite modifications had been carried out on the plane that crashed near Paris. In fact, no such modifications had been made. Moreover, the paperwork relating to another DC-10 supplied to the now defunct Laker Airways proved to be similarly misleading. It is unclear precisely how the paperwork was produced. What is certain is that the Airworthiness Directives that would have compelled the requisite modifications were withdrawn following a 'gentleman's agreement' between the president of McDonnell-Douglas and the chief of staff of the regional Federal Aviation Authority, whereby McDonnell-Douglas undertook to fix the 'goddam plane'. In fact all that happened was some 'beefing up' of the electric wiring on the door followed by service bulletins recommending more changes to the door-locking mechanism. The bulletins were issued among scores of others without any indication that these were life and death matters.

In other words, the disaster happened because the chief of McDonnell-Douglas used his relationship with the regional aviation chief to negotiate a concession that avoided having the planes withdrawn from service. It happened because the regional aviation chief had become so identified with the industry that he was willing to stretch a point to the extent of allowing DC-10s to continue in service with potentially lethal design faults (Evans 1983).

While Barings never abused the concession granted by the Bank of England in the way that McDonnell-Douglas exploited the 'gentlemen's agreement', it certainly made use of it. Uzzi (1999) suggests that beyond a certain threshold embeddedness can undermine economic performance by making organizations vulnerable to exogenous shocks or insulating them from information that exists beyond their network. The flexibility accorded to Barings again meant that another of the checks and balances in the system was disconnected. Moreover, the Bank of England's expression of trust may have been taken by Barings as confirmation of its competence, rendering Barings less sensitive to negative feedback such as market rumour than it might otherwise have been.

Management information

Recall that action generators reflect what the organization sees as important (Starbuck 1983). MANCO's action generators mainly focused upon reported revenues. MANCO did not receive nor did it request any proper analysis of risk. Andrew Tuckey did not receive or request a copy of the internal audit report (Secretary of State versus Tuckey). Nor did MANCO attempt to track the amount of margin posted or ask for information on the precise number of contracts being traded. Attention was focused on what seemed important, that is, earnings.

Consequently within the programmed domain, everything appeared to be working well. That observation, however, applied only to the programmed domain (Starbuck 1983) and even that was wrong because the reported revenues were fictitious.

The illusion of control

While the aforementioned action generators contributed to Barings' demise by helping to mask potentially ominous developments, the data suggest that psychological and social influences were also at work. Recall that theories of self-enhancement posit that we typically see ourselves as superior to others while underestimating the impact of contributions made by others. Peter Barings' reference in 1993 made six months after Heath's forced departure to the 'amazing recovery' in the securities business is tinged with hostility – a fainter echo of the behaviour of the two Nobel Prize winners. It is also ego defensive as Peter Baring is suggesting that Christopher Heath and his colleagues were wrong in their assessment of the prospects in markets in the Far East. The comment also implies that Heath was dispensable. The apparent recovery showed that Heath had no monopoly of knowledge and talent after all. Anyone could make money in the securities business provided they were in the right place at the right time. Barings' senior managers might have been jealous of Heath's success and irked by the pointed allusions to the 'pisspot' merchant bank and, as Stein (2000) suggests, anxious following his departure. Leeson's apparent profits clearly suggested that the securities business had a future. Those profits may even have been taken as confirmation that Barings had been right all along in its decision to diversify.

It also meant a wrong assessment of risk. Applying Sitkin and Pablo's (1992) definition of risk, expected outcomes were assumed to be fairly certain and 'not terribly difficult' to achieve and that it was therefore unlikely that potential outcomes could involve extreme consequences – even though Heath's organization did ultimately lose money and through propriety trading that Barings was unaware of at the time. In theory we would expect such behaviour from decision-makers with high risk propensity. What happens in this book contradicts Sitkin and Pablo's theory as Peter Baring and other members of MANCO rationalize the risks involved in Leeson's alleged trading to fit their self-image as risk averse *and* cleverer than the competition that have yet to discover the opportunities in Singapore.

Potentially another consequence of Peter Barings' comment to the Bank of England would be psychological 'lock-in'. That is, norms for consistency would dictate that having formed an explanation for something, we stick to it and rationalize subsequent developments to fit the explanation. Members of MANCO succumb to reasoning by analogy as they decide that Leeson's continuing success is history repeating itself. This was a crucial error of judgement because they subsequently rationalize new information to fit the framework. By November 1994 they have decided that the business must decline as competitors move in. Then in 1995 when Leeson's profits begin to outstrip those of the entire organization, they do not see the situation as too good to be true, but far too good to last. Their attention becomes focused upon building new business for the future rather than questioning events of the present.

Legally Mr Tuckey had a duty to ensure that matters coming before the Management Committee were properly considered (Secretary of State versus Tuckey). Recall the imposition of trading limits implied risk. Moreover, the huge profits being generated latterly strongly suggested that those limits were being broken. It is a matter of record that those issues were never explored by MANCO. When challenged in court to suggest how trading could benefit from 'volatility being crushed', Tuckey was unable to offer a satisfactory explanation. 'I cannot say I am surprised,' said the judge, 'it is complete gobbledygook to me.'

Nor did any other member of MANCO question the statement. We will never know whether such incurious behaviour reflected complacency or fear of appearing foolish. It may well have been a combination of both.

Groupthink

We can eliminate polarization and risky shift as explanations for poor decision-making by MANCO because a precondition of both phenomena is that the group discusses the issues before reaching a decision. MANCO was not the kind of decision-making forum where issues get thrashed out.

Pearl Harbor was the last thing the American military were expecting. The key difference between events of 1941 and Barings' collapse is that Janis's (1982) model of groupthink was developed to explain decision errors made by groups well aware that they were facing acute danger whereas Barings was oblivious. Yet MANCO's behaviour is consistent with some of the features of groupthink. More specifically, although MANCO was not as cohesive as some of the policy-making groups studied by Janis, there was nevertheless a significant level of cohesion among members as evidenced by the longevity of the group (most members had known one another for years), the stability of membership and the fact that inter-personal tensions were not allowed to impinge on the conduct of business. While MANCO was not as insulated as the groups studied by Janis, as all directors had departmental responsibilities and some were also members of ALCO, nonetheless they were relatively remote from the realities of day-to-day operations. Certainly the mannered weekly meetings contrasted sharply with the clamour and coarseness of the trading pit. Like the groups studied by Janis (1982), there were few norms requiring methodical decision-making procedures. For instance, there were no rigorous and detailed protocols for monitoring risk.

Consistent with Janis's research, ALCO served as a kind of 'mind-guard' as evidenced by the anodyne reporting of the SLK transaction, the repeated assurances that Leeson's positions were matched, and portraying Leeson's latter-day profits in a manner calculated to appeal to self-enhancement, that is as resulting from volatile market conditions that Barings had been clever enough to exploit. Unlike the role played by Robert Kennedy in frustrating wiser counsels, however, in theory any member of the group could have challenged these explanations.

In practice, it was culturally forbidden for group members to question one another. When challenged in court about the degree of trust that the members of MANCO reposed in one another, Tuckey replied:

> It was not our practice with senior colleagues to interrogate them as to what steps they had actually taken to bring themselves into a state of confidence and satisfaction . . . Our culture was particularly inconsistent with that.
>
> (Secretary of State versus Tuckey)

It was this more than anything else that undermined the advantages of group decision-making. Since self-censorship occurs unconsciously, its existence cannot be proved. What can be said is that the group's reaction to market rumour is consistent with extreme self-censorship and consequent illusion of invulnerability. Never for one moment does the group consider the possibility of 'no smoke without fire'. Moreover, given that *everything* depended upon positions being matched, the group could have asked Peter Norris to check. Asking the question carried no risk of ego damage but it did require a willingness to believe in the possibility that Barings might not be invulnerable. Yes, it meant violating group norms by asking what measures Norris had taken to bring himself into a state of satisfaction that positions were matched. Yes, the culture may have been 'particularly inconsistent with that' but here was an extreme situation calling for a vigorous response.

Another lost opportunity was Diarmid Kelly's observation about concomitant risk. Kelly made this comment on 6 February 1995. If it had been acted on promptly, the bank might have been saved, albeit severely damaged. Kelly meets a brick wall because again such discussion would have required members to challenge one another and the cultural norms of the group are 'particularly inconsistent' with that. Instead the members of the Management Committee stick to their self-serving rationalization of deeming Leeson's trading to be 'essentially without risk' (Secretary of State versus Tuckey).

Pfeffer (1992) argues that it is easy for a strong culture to produce groupthink. This is because a strong culture means that group members share a common set of goals. They are also imbued with a common perspective on what to do and how to accomplish it and a common vocabulary that allows them to coordinate their behaviour. Those factors can create pressure to conform to the dominant view.

According to the media and popular press, the dominant view of MANCO centred on greed. They were certainly surrounded by a culture of greed as far as the securities business was concerned. (Leeson is alleged to have celebrated his birthday by putting his gold American Express card on a bar counter and then claiming it had been stolen: Pharo 1995; see also Economist 1995a, 1995b, 1995c.) They also had their own bonuses to consider. Peter Baring's remuneration for 1993 was over £1 million and Andrew Tuckey's was nearly £2 million (Treasury Committee, 15 May 1996: 25). Moreover, experts confirm that, excluding Leeson's activities and the investment management activities, the bank was possibly losing money and was certainly hugely unprofitable even in good years (Treasury Committee, Minutes of Evidence, 31 January 1996: 7). Intuitively we might think that that knowledge discouraged whistle blowing. Yet MANCO members' willingness to approve ALCO's instruction to Leeson not to increase positions suggests that they were not completely driven by greed. Moreover, they were sensitive to the adverse reaction in the market – perhaps fearing they were becoming too clever for their own good. It is a speculative point, but MANCO may have been afraid that just as when Bunker Hunt tried to corner the silvers market, prompting the Chicago Metals Exchange to change the rules by limiting how many contracts members could hold thereby destroying Hunt (see Abolafia and Kilduff 1988), that SIMEX and Osaka might behave in a similarly arbitrary manner. MANCO members thought they were behaving responsibly and managing risk, but like ALCO they were focusing on the wrong risks.

16 Summary and conclusions

According to the eminent social-psychologist Karl Weick (1993, 1995), while it may not take much to become an organization, it may not take much to stop being one either. For Barings' directors and employees, the sudden collapse of the organization was like a car crash. One minute they were bowling along. The next their lives were shattered (Gapper and Pirie 2005).

Before discussing the implications of this book for theory and practice, it may be helpful to briefly summarize key events of the story. Leeson's career with Barings might have been extremely short-lived if the false statement made on his licence application had been investigated or if actors in Singapore had checked with London instead of merely 'rubber stamping' the form. Once ensconced in Singapore, it took just three strokes on a computer keyboard and completion of a simple form to create the secret account that Leeson used to hide his illicit trading. Details of that account turned up on a suspense file in London but the file was never audited.

Leeson's role in Singapore involved executing contracts to buy or sell at specified prices on behalf of colleagues based in Japan. Leeson made numerous mistakes learning the job, which he temporarily held in the secret account while waiting for the market to move in his favour. Strictly speaking this constituted propriety trading, which was against the rules, but it was common practice in Barings though not to the extent essayed by Leeson. In addition, Leeson began underpricing business in order to impress his colleagues in Japan. He hid the resultant loss in the secret account. Leeson's colleagues were unaware of his antics because, unlike in Japan where contract prices are displayed on computer screens, SIMEX is an open outcry market. Consequently they never knew what price Leeson actually obtained. Moreover, since Leeson became virtually self-supervising, there was no one sufficiently close to him in Singapore to see what he was doing.

Self-supervision was not what Barings intended. The fax setting out the arrangements for controlling Leeson provided for two supervisors, one named Gordon Bowser, who was based in London, and the other was Simon Jones based in Singapore. As James Bax, Barings' Area Manager for the Far East, predicted, however, the result was a disaster for Barings as dual supervision became 'no supervision'.

Eventually the losses became so large that Leeson began trying to trade his way back into profit. He sold financial contracts known as options that attracted large sums in premium which were booked as profit. Since those contracts depended upon the Nikkei index remaining virtually stable, Leeson's losses almost invariably exceeded the premium received, forcing him to sell more and more options. This made him seem very successful when in reality he was exposing Barings to more and more risk.

Leeson was free to trade with impunity because not only was he unsupervised, but also he was responsible for the paperwork associated with settling trades. As both poacher and gamekeeper, Leeson could 'fiddle' prices, move between bank accounts and so on. Leeson had no authority to sell options. He covered his tracks by pretending that he had discovered highly profitable opportunities for arbitrage trading, for example, buying a quantity in Singapore and immediately selling on in Osaka for a higher price.

By late 1993 Leeson's apparently profitable arbitrage business was beginning to have a noticeable impact on the balance sheet. Peter Baring saw the figures and assumed that Barings Securities was on the road to recovery following a depressed period when adverse market conditions coupled with (allegedly) poor leadership had led to substantial losses. By the end of 1994 Leeson was firmly established as Barings' star trader. In fact he was concealing losses of around £200 million.

There were signs that all was not well in Singapore. In July 1992 Barings noticed that it appeared to have paid out £10 million more than it had received from customers. By mid-1994 the unreconciled balance was over £90 million and rising. Moreover, Leeson was calling upon London to pay out millions of pounds in collateral (margin) to support his trading, but proved reluctant to explain precisely how the money was being used. The chronic reconciliation problem is just one of the issues that the internal auditors were asked to examine when they visited Singapore in mid-1994. The audit could have exposed Leeson's unauthorized trading but it misses the mark.

Barley and Tolbert (1986; see also Greener 2006) suggest that the trigger for institutions like apartheid and communism to collapse is when disparate and disconnected actors start to alter their behaviour and start moving in concert until a kind of 'tipping point' is reached whereby movement gathers pace and eventually becomes unstoppable just as an epidemic of a disease may suddenly become a pandemic (e.g. Gladwell 2000). Latterly something akin to this happened in Barings as other powerful actors move to support Leeson when it is discovered that he has apparently sold options worth £50 million 'over the counter' to a firm of brokers whose credit-worthiness is unknown. Not only has Leeson no authority to conduct such a sale, but also he has apparently forgotten to collect payment. The incident is virtually 'brushed under the carpet' partly because senior managers want to avoid upsetting their star trader but also to detract attention from their own failures. In fact there was no sum of money owing. The missing £50 million was a portion of Leeson's losses.

By late January/early February 1995 Barings has over £500 million in margin posted to Singapore – more than the bank's entire capital base of about £480 million.

No one was worried because it was understood that Leeson's trades were matched. For example, that a contract to buy a quantity in Singapore was matched by an equal and opposite contract in Japan. This assumption was false but it was never checked.

Latterly financial markets in the Far East were ablaze with rumours suggesting Barings was overexposed to a customer. Instead of investigating those rumours or even pausing to think whether there was 'no smoke without fire', Barings merely assumed that because one exchange published positions and the other did not, that the market was seeing only half of the equation. When Leeson's profits escalated dramatically in late January 1995 following the Kobe earthquake, Peter Baring became alarmed not because Leeson's profits seemed too good to be true, but because they seemed to be too good to last. It was surely only a matter of time before competitors awoke to the possibilities.

Meanwhile, Barings saw what it expected to see, namely escalating margin calls while Leeson's continuing to account for those funds was rationalized as symptomatic of the chaos that has developed through Leeson trying to do two jobs, trading and settlement. A junior employee named Tony Railton was seconded to Singapore to disentangle the mess. Railton grappled for three weeks with Leeson's accounts. Finally he gave up, assuming that he must have missed something that only Leeson could explain. It was only when Leeson mysteriously disappeared that the alarm was finally raised.

Implications for organizational research

Investment banks have learned lessons from Barings' collapse. Many have implemented highly sophisticated systems to manage risk and measure the amount of capital at risk at a given moment. Legal and compliance functions have been strengthened. A former Barings Securities executive is quoted in the *Financial Times* newspaper as saying, 'Compliance officers were office boys who you could tell to fuck off if you were on the phone to a client . . . Now they run the business' (Larsen 2005a). International regulation has also been bolstered.

Such developments raise questions for research. One question is whether instituting more systems of control actually increases risk and danger by making it more likely that administering the system becomes an end in itself and also more likely that a 'tick box' mentality develops. Moreover, tightening systems can create operational problems, for example, if staff are needed urgently but have to undergo lengthy security checks. The literature on symbols and organizational legitimacy (e.g. Pfeffer 1981) implies that the trappings of control like compliance and clinical governance (see below) exist to make us think we are safe by surrounding organizations with an aura of respectability. In order to explore this disturbing but by no mean implausible possibility, we need to know more about how such procedures are operated in practice. For example, we know that gaps almost invariably exist between theory and practice but just how wide do they become, when, where and under what circumstances?

How are rules enforced in practice, what leeway is given and what do employees get away with? Do compliance officers really 'run the place' and if so to what effect? It was suggested in Chapter 3 that bureaucratic mechanisms need to be supported by a disciplined control culture in organizations. The assumption that cultural change can reduce the likelihood of malfeasance has yet to be empirically verified however. Leeson (1996) may have been correct in suggesting that he would never have been able to create a secret error account in a more disciplined organization like his former employers Morgan Stanley. What are the defining features of such cultures? For example, do they utilize more elaborate control structures and if so, how do they avoid the tendency for control to negate control? Alternatively do they rely more upon so-called loose/tight mechanisms of control, that is, few rules but tightly enforced? Do such cultures encourage compliance officers to distinguish between the letter of the law and the spirit? If we believe what we read in newspapers, investment banks still tend to look favourably on units that generate large profits and are mainly interested in being *seen* to comply with the rules (e.g. Larsen 2005b).

Such research has implications for other organizational activities including the elaborate procedures for clinical governance established since Harold Shipman. Such procedures are designed to protect patient safety by ensuring, for example, that only properly qualified and registered personnel are employed and that they remain competent to do their jobs. It is beyond the scope of this book to judge their effectiveness. The question is, does the introduction of such mechanisms promote a cultural change in organizations, or would a cultural change render them redundant, or do organizations need a combination of cultural and formal structural control and if so what emphasis should be given to each?

This book has implications for what we regard as worth researching in organization theory. Strategy captures the limelight at the expense of considering more mundane ways in which organizations change. Mundanity is an illusion. As Feldman (2000) predicts, slight almost imperceptible structural shifts like ceasing to specify prices can lead to disaster. If we focus all our attention upon strategy, we may miss other factors that can significantly affect the fate of an organization. Research might focus upon elucidating prototypical models of change and 'what leads to what'.

Implications for research in psychology of risk

Investment banks are now more inclined to question success as well as failure (Larsen 2005a). It is unclear, however, whether they actually examine success as rigorously as they examine failure? Recall that Dunegan (1993) observed that when feedback was negative (bottle perceived as half-empty), decisions were subject to much more critical scrutiny than when the bottle was perceived as half-full. What happens when the bottle is nine-tenths full or even overflowing? For instance, systems of clinical governance highlight unusual death rates, but does anyone think to take a closer look at apparently very successful doctors and see what might lie behind the statistics?

Arguably preferences do not guide action but emerge as a result of taking action (Weick 1979). Yet Barings maintained its professed low risk propensity to the end. In theory, therefore, we would have expected Barings to have been fearful of even the relatively low risks involved in arbitrage (Sitkin and Pablo 1992). A plausible explanation for this discrepancy between theory and evidence is that risk propensity is mediated by outcome expectancy (Wong 2005). Leeson's sustained success may have suggested that substantial returns from arbitrage were almost guaranteed. Such high outcome expectancy may have made actors like Peter Baring more inclined to accept the risk on a risk/reward basis. Yet since there is no evidence that they ever weighed up the two factors, a more plausible possibility is that high outcome expectancy can result in decision-makers subjectively redefining the level of risk so that it matches their risk-taking propensity – a much more dangerous possibility. A more recent parallel is Cadbury's refining their criterion of what constitutes 'safe' or 'acceptable' levels of contamination.

Shadow option

The expected pay-off from Leeson's alleged arbitrage went beyond immediate returns. The possibility of developing the business represented what economists call a shadow option, namely one that grew out of existing activities (Janney and Dess 2004). Recall that an option confers the right but not the obligation to do something in the future if specified conditions apply. Options can be defined more generally as toehold investments that enable organizations to eliminate uncertainty. For example, an organization may decide to purchase a marginal oilfield but to commence drilling only if oil rises above a certain price to make drilling economically worthwhile – known as a delayed entry option. Options are controversial as it has been argued that they can produce suboptimal decisions (Zardkoohi 2004). For example, the owner of a failing business may decide to wait a year and see how things go before deciding whether to close it down – known as a delayed exit option. In fact all they may be doing is postponing the evil day and wasting time, money and energy in the process.

In Barings' case the shadow option appeared to remove uncertainty because it meant that Barings had less to fear from competitors muscling in on Singapore. Significantly shadow means 'nothing'. A question for research is whether and to what extent the emergence of an attractive shadow option may cause decision-makers to overvalue the activity from which the option has emerged. In other words, would the Management Committee have been more worried if there had been *less* at stake?

Passive escalation

Judging by reports of their demeanour, Peter Baring and Andrew Tuckey leaned more towards 'Type B' than 'Type A' personality profiles, that is, relatively relaxed, more confident, and less openly competitive than so-called Type A individuals. For example, Tuckey said in court that if he had known around mid-February 1995 that Barings had over £500 million posted in margin calls, he would have been 'surprised'. The trial judge contradicted him and said that he should have been extremely alarmed. Schaubroeck and Williams (1993) observed that so-called Type A personalities were more prone to escalation than so-called Type B personalities, possibly because of the former's greater need for achievement striving than their more sanguine counterparts. This book suggests that Type Bs may be prone to escalation but in a different way. That is, whereas Type A personalities are likely to actively reinvest in failing decisions, Type B personalities may be more of a liability in situations where decisions to reinvest can be made passively – such as via the routine payment of margin calls.

Traders' option

Evidence suggests that individuals with a high need for achievement or who hail from cultural backgrounds where individual achievement is at a premium are more likely to become 'rogue traders' by escalating their losses than their less self-centred counterparts (e.g. Moon 2001). Future studies might also explore whether such behaviours are gender related. Is it just a coincidence that 'rogue traders' are usually men?

Leeson's behaviour is consistent with experiments that have shown that anxious individuals are more likely to escalate their commitment than depressed individuals (Moon et al. 2003). Latterly Leeson (1996) became ill with anxiety, consuming kilos of boiled sweets to calm his nerves, and was prone to bouts of sweating and vomiting as he feared exposure at any moment. There is another pattern of behaviour that can affect highly stressed individuals known as 'threat rigidity', which as the term suggests renders them incapable of taking decisions and acting (Staw et al. 1981). It is a speculative point but possibly depressed as distinct from anxious individuals may be more prone to threat rigidity than escalation. It is an important issue because in certain situations threat rigidity may produce catastrophe. For example, military leaders are taught that when under fire it is better to make a decision, even if it is the wrong one, than to make no decision at all.

A problem now recognized by investment banks is known as 'trader's option', whereby success is rewarded by bigger bonuses and failure by dismissal. 'Once a trader has suffered sufficient losses *to lose his job*, there is little incentive not to take on greater risks in an attempt to get out of trouble' (Larsen 2005a: 3, italics added). This book suggests that it is dangerous to assume that losses have to be sufficiently serious to warrant outright dismissal to prompt risk-seeking behaviour. The errors that Leeson made mastering execution were miniscule relative to his later losses, but he hid them for fear of demotion. More research is needed to ascertain what level of definite loss is sufficient to engender risk-seeking behaviour. It would not be surprising to discover that the prospect of the merest loss, material or psychological may suffice.

Malfeasance as water

A decade after the collapse, Peter Norris told the *Financial Times* newspaper: 'It's ludicrous . . . to presume that systems and processes have moved on such that it's not a concern any more. There's something about the nature of wholesale financial markets that makes it impossible to control these sorts of events' (Larsen 2005a: 3). If we cannot control them we may at least be able to better anticipate that 'something' by how we conceptualize malfeasance. I want to suggest that the image of water can help us to grasp the nature of the threat of malfeasance and generate insight into where and how the threat may emerge.

Before elaborating on this idea, it is necessary to briefly explain the role of metaphor in organization theory and behaviour (further discussed in Morgan 1980; see also Brown 1977; Morgan 1996). A metaphor is a linguistic device whereby one phenomenon is understood in terms of another. The notion of a computer possessing a 'memory', for example, enables us to conceptualize its storage capabilities, while the notion of 'virus' highlights the potentially contagious nature of computer malfunctioning.

Metaphors highlight points of correspondence between one phenomenon and another. Yet correspondence can never be total, otherwise the metaphor would be redundant. For example, to suggest 'software is like software' illuminates nothing. Yet to say that software is the 'engine' that drives the system facilitates a rudimentary grasp of the role of computer programs. Metaphors are inherently partial, therefore. They illuminate certain features of a phenomenon while obscuring others. For instance, the notion of the mind as a 'machine' highlights the mind's reasoning and analytical powers but eclipses other capabilities of mind such as intuition and creativity. Metaphors are not only linguistic devices to make the task of reading more interesting, but also the basic means whereby people develop an understanding of the world. Indeed, all knowledge is metaphorical. For example, notions of 'time' and 'consciousness' exist only as metaphors. Yet metaphors do not exist as absolutes. They are basically human constructions used to facilitate understanding.

The choice of metaphor is crucial because it determines how a problem is perceived. For example, madness can be seen as an illness requiring hospitalization and cure, or as measure of social distance. Some metaphors are so commonplace that we seldom think about them. For example, the concept of time is almost automatically linked to the notion of 'clock'. Likewise, when we think of memory we almost automatically equate it with the notion of repository. Metaphors may help us to understand our world but they can also constrain our understanding because our assumptions become bounded by the choice of metaphor. The eminent physicist Stephen Hawking realized that theory and research in physics was bounded by the notion of the clock which depicts time as moving forwards. This insight prompted Hawking to reconceptualize time as moving backwards as well as forwards and hence to the 'discovery' of so-called 'black holes'. Likewise, the assumption that memory tells us what has happened obscures another important but counterintuitive possibility, namely that memory tells us what is *going* to happen.

There are two types of metaphor, analogue and iconic. An analogue tells you what something is *like*, for example, 'a woman without a man is like a fish without a bicycle'. In contrast an iconic metaphor tells you what something *is*.

For example, a statute and a photograph are iconic metaphors. In practice all metaphors are analogue and iconic. The distinction is made because the two forms of metaphor fulfil different functions. An analogue metaphor facilitates *comp*rehension whereas an iconic metaphor facilitates *app*rehension (Brown 1977).

Gerald Mars' intellectually rigorous but highly accessible book named *Cheats at Work* (1982) uses animal imagery to depict how opportunists prey on organizations. The image of malfeasance as water has been developed as complementary to Mars' work, mainly to facilitate apprehension, that is, to envisage malfeasance in action. It may also help us to comprehend why Peter Norris is correct in warning us against over-reliance upon systems and procedures to prevent and detect malfeasance.

Imagining water

Water finds the lowest level. Imagine a small pool of water in the lowest deck of a boat. It should not be there but it is and, unless the pool suddenly expands, people may cease to notice it. The £10 million reconciliation problem discovered in Barings in late 1992 was an aberration, but it became a fact of life even as the sum involved gradually grew larger. The image of water as 'staying low' also implies that malfeasance on a small scale may well go undetected. For example, in a butcher's shop assistants can steal money just by leaving fat on the meat that would otherwise be accounted for as waste when meat is trimmed at the point of sale. Provided miscreants 'stay low', that is, are not greedy they may get away with it indefinitely – particularly if they are not closely supervised. Likewise almost all organizations have reconciliation problems, sometimes dating back years. Those balances may be written off because of the sheer cost of pursuing a 'cold' reconciliation trail relative to the amount involved. Again miscreants are unlikely to be caught unless they get greedy.

The lowest level of the boat is usually the least frequented area. Likewise, the most dangerous parts of the organization may be the outposts like Singapore, the less glamorous departments and the dark corners that no one is interested in where suspense files dwell and where water can accumulate and stagnate unnoticed.

Water is a soft yielding force. Its most distinctive property is that it shapes itself to its surroundings. Water can therefore penetrate the fault lines in organizational control structures and eventually split them wide open. Dual supervision is one example. Another was the facility to create new accounts on the computer. The fault line at the institutional level was technological: one exchange published details of trades, the other did not.

Water imagery helps us anticipate how miscreants can evade elaborate systems of checks and balances by simply flowing round them. For instance, when Leeson is pressed by Treasury staff in London to supply proper accounts, he sometimes makes vague promises, never argues and cheerfully continues faxing margin calls. Nor does he argue when he is instructed not to increase positions. He just carries on. Flowing round controls can mean that malfeasance is off the radar screen. For instance, a group of rogue traders nicknamed the Flaming Ferraris after the cocktails they drank were banned for life from working in the City for illicit trading (Mackintosh 2001). The group used mobile phones in order to circumnavigate controls whereby telephone calls are routinely recorded and monitored in investment banks. Likewise, Leeson flows round the controls when he quietly omits to connect account 88888 to reporting systems.

Water erodes and corrodes. Given time it can wear down mighty boulders. Eventually settlements staff in London virtually gave up trying to procure more detailed information from Leeson. Where delay is harmful to the other party, actors can manipulate control over time to wear the other party down. Leeson wore the auditors down with his complex explanations of how he made his profits, taking a tick here, crossing a leg there, thus forcing them to moderate their demands. Leeson also manipulated control over time to wear the external auditors down by increasing the pressure to meet the deadline for getting the accounts signed off.

Water may be soft and yielding but it can become a torrent hurling everything from its path. Water achieves such power by assuming a particular configuration. By making himself useful, by turning the values of private appropriation against his employers, Leeson turned from a trickle into a torrent and eventually dominated Barings, forcing aside the internal auditor's more dangerous recommendations, overriding Hawes, breaking SIMEX rules and so forth.

The destabilizing effects of water are perhaps most dangerous when they are invisible. Leeson's licence applications would probably survive the disciplinary gaze of an audit because procedures were followed in London and appeared to have been followed in Singapore. The only criticism would probably have been not replying to the FSA promptly. The flow of margin out of London was like a stream running under a house. Metaphorically speaking it eventually undermined the foundations of the building bringing the walls crashing down.

A metaphor's value lies in either prompting us to think differently about the familiar, for example the notion of organizations as 'psychic prisons' (Morgan 1996), or the metaphor's resonance with a particular phenomenon. Resonance in turn depends upon the number of connections that can be generated from the metaphor. For instance, one metaphor I thought of was that of malfeasance as like a sewer rat, scuttling unseen below the surface and much more prevalent than we might expect. The metaphor has its uses but it does not suggest as many connections as water.

The particular resonance of water imagery is that it enables us to apprehend what Allison and Zelikow (1999: xii) call 'the awesome crack' that may reside between the impossible and the improbable. It was not impossible that someone who was not a fit and proper person to be licensed could slip through the net but how probable did it appear? It was not impossible that someone could set up a bogus account but surely they would be caught? There was indeed a 'significant general risk' that controls could be overridden by the general manager but how probable did that risk seem?

Implications for practice

This final section of the book focuses on two questions:

- How can organizations prevent or at least detect malfeasance sooner rather than later?
- How can organizations reduce the risk of decision error?

We begin by reviewing some of the lessons adduced by the Board of Banking Supervision (1995):

> Perhaps the clearest lesson that emerges from the Barings' collapse is that institutions must recognise the dangers of not segregating responsibility for 'front office' and 'back office' functions. Clear segregation of duties is a fundamental principle of internal control in all businesses and has long been recognised as the first line of protection against the risk of fraudulent or unauthorised activities. *In the exceptional case of segregation of duties not being feasible due, for example, to the small size of the operation*, controls must be established such that they compensate for the increased risk this brings.
>
> (Board of Banking Supervision 1995: 254, italics added)

Segregation is a sensible precaution but why make exceptions? In Barings' case the Singapore office was so small that it would probably have qualified for exemption. The additional controls (dual supervision) might have seemed adequate on paper but in practice proved ineffective. There is an issue of public policy here. Barings was not a victimless crime. Bondholders, many of them elderly and living on fixed incomes, lost their life savings when ING refused them compensation (Gapper and Denton 1996). If a small business owner wants to sell cooked and raw food, they must employ two staff regardless of turnover. Why should investment banks with their much greater resources be any different? Allowing exceptions creates the kind of flexibility that malfeasance loves.

The Board of Banking Supervision (1995: 253) also said: 'Clearly defined lines of responsibility and accountability . . . must be established and all employees informed of the reporting structure.'

More specifically, organizations should:

> Maintain an up-to-date organizational chart which shows clearly all reporting lines and who is accountable to whom and for what. There must be no room for confusion . . . Every individual should have a job description which clearly identifies his or her responsibilities and to whom or for what he or she is accountable.
>
> (Board of Banking Supervision 1995: 253)

While it would be folly to suggest that organizations should not do these things, a lesson that emerges from this book is that role clarity is a necessary but insufficient condition of organizational effectiveness. There is always room for confusion, ambiguity always lurks.

Describing structure as a figment of imagination qua Giddens (1979, 1984) might strike practising mangers as ridiculous. Indeed, although Peter Norris fully accepted responsibility for his part in the collapse, he has nevertheless always insisted that reporting lines were clear (e.g. Treasury Committee, 10 June 1996: 45). The point is, while managers can specify structure, they need to allow for the subtly shifting tides of organization. Just as the Chinese proverb states that we can never set foot in the same river twice, it is important to remember that organizations exist in a constant state of flux and transformation. Consequently, there may be a considerable discrepancy between the organization that exists in the minds of managers and the structure that evolves as a result of 'normal' daily patterned interaction.

While organizations need clear and simple rules, they should also recognize that rules cannot exert control – only people can do that. It is important to recognize, moreover, that although in theory rules guide action, in practice rules *emerge* from action (Weick 1979). Instead of imagining employees as rule bound it is safer to think of them as forever inventing the rules of relevance and irrelevance as, for example, in the handling of Leeson's licence application to the FSA. In plain language managers should know what goes on in their organizations.

The missing hero

While it is important that managers define responsibilities of employees, they must recognize that responsibility only really exists where it is accepted, otherwise there is no responsibility. Leeson's reporting lines were perfectly clear. Yet as James Bax predicted, the arrangement proved disastrous because no one took responsibility for overseeing his activities.

The same goes for authority. According to the Board of Banking Supervision (1995), Barings collapsed because key individuals failed to do their jobs. While this statement may be factually correct, it fails to acknowledge the obstacles that people like Tony Hawes and Ian Hopkins faced. Hopkins, for instance, bitterly contested the ban imposed by the FSA, arguing that he had done his level best to highlight weaknesses in controls (e.g. Gapper 1997; see also Treasury Committee, 23 July 1996). Responsibility and authority do not always match in organizations. It may sound weak in a court of law for an employee to say, 'I knew I would be wasting my time' or 'I would only be marked down as a trouble maker' or 'I tried but no one would listen'. Yet when employees fail in their duties, it is rarely because they are lazy or incompetent but usually because of the restraints imposed by informal cues and unhelpful behaviours of other actors.

A lesson for practice lies in how managers conceptualize authority. Authority is not something that can be doled out from on high. Nor is it something that an individual can possess. Genuine authority is a relationship based upon mutual respect for the legitimate needs of the parties to that relationship (Knights and Roberts 1982). Bonus systems like the one operated by Barings can be destructive because they encourage the pursuit of individual interest – rather like the tragedy of the commons. The commons were stretches of lands offering free grazing rights. Logically this presents an invitation to the peasant to graze one more beast. Ultimately the pursuit of individual interest results in collective ruin of the land (Hardin 1968; see also Platt 1973). Managers have a duty to acknowledge the tension that inevitably exists between the pursuit of profit and control of risk and to seek to resolve it. Hawes should have been able to say to Peter Norris, 'Without the cooperation of XYZ I cannot do my job,' and been taken seriously.

The Board of Banking Supervision enjoins organizations to address bad relationships. It is good advice. Imagine a steam locomotive with leaking pistons. The engine can still pull trains but only at reduced efficiency. Bad relationships can have a similar effect. That is, since organizations realize their productive potential through cooperation between actors, any breakdown in relations such as that which occurred between Geoff Broadhurst and Simon Jones and between Ron Baker and Tony Hawes is likely to undermine the power of the organization. Incidentally malfeasance may test relationships because the outcroppings may suggest that people are failing to do their jobs properly. For example, when the alleged SLK transaction was first reported to London, Barings lambasted the external auditors for employing an idiot on the accounts (Gapper and Denton 1996).

That said, good relations should not be purchased at the price of suppressing conflict. One of the big 'if only's' of the story occurred on 6 February 1995 when Diarmid Kelly doubted Leeson's reported $9 million risk-free profits for the week but was ignored. The lesson is that while conflict can be destabilizing, there is a price to be paid for suppressing it. Conflict may seem like an obstacle but it is actually a *trans*action (Brown 1977; see also Edelman 1971) that enables a range of mindsets and information to be brought to bear upon a problem. If conflict is stifled, part of the synergy of group membership may be lost. Kelly was adding value to the discussion but for all the notice that was taken, he might as well have been absent.

In an influential article Tom Peters (1978) pointed out that executives don't drive trucks or serve customers (or trade financial contracts) but deal primarily in symbols. According to Peters one of the most powerful symbolic acts in organizations is how managers spend their time. Employees use this information to deduce what is actually as important regardless of what managerial rhetoric might suggest. When actors in key positions do not take time to read, say, an internal audit report, employees draw the obvious conclusion.

Recognizing signs of malfeasance

Stein (2000) argues that Leeson left numerous clues to his activities as a result of an unconscious desire to be caught. A more prosaic possibility is that he could hardly have done otherwise as financial irregularities usually reveal themselves somewhere in 'the system'. The lesson for practice is that the outcroppings of fraud may be missed precisely because they make 'no sense'. They may reside, for example, in the boxes of computer printout marked 'garbage' that find their ways into the corners of organizations and end up gathering dust. Or they may be flung into suspense files because 'the system' keeps rejecting the data. Such apparent 'glitches' should be investigated, particularly if they suddenly occur in a mature information system.

Thinking ahead

In 1991, a detective told an international conference on fraud and white-collar crime in Liverpool:

> A clerk working in a local council education office wanted to visit her daughter in Australia. Lacking the necessary financial means to make the trip, she decided that as they already had 367 schools in the borough they [the council] wouldn't notice if they had another – and for three years they didn't.

The clerk used the computer to create a fictitious school and then diverted the salary payments into her personal bank account. Although it took more than three key strokes to create a new school, it proved surprisingly easy.

The challenge for management is to try and anticipate how such mundane facilities as access to computer screens might be used creatively by potential fraudsters. In addition, while organizations cannot dispense with programmed decisions like the automatic payment of margin calls, systems designers should consider how such triggers could harm the organization, and incorporate safeguards. For instance, if the 'system' had begun to reject Leeson's margin calls when they reached a certain level, the resultant crisis would have forced Barings to focus on the problem. Had that happened it would have heightened awareness of the unaccounted for quantum posted without any credit checks upon Leeson's mystery customer.

Solution first: problem later

Recall that for key actors like Peter Norris and Ron Baker, the most shocking aspect of the bank's collapse was the gap that existed between what they understood and believed to be true and the reality (e.g. Treasury Committee, 23 July 1996b: 97). What occurred highlights the dangers of moving into solution mode too quickly and giving insufficient time to reflecting upon the precise nature of the problem. Problems such as a strained overdraft facility and market rumour may seem self-evident but they rarely are.

Fine-tuning the odds

One function of the trope of irony is to expose differences in things that appear similar and similarities in things that appear different (Brown 1977). Ostensibly comparisons between an aristocratic merchant bank and London Underground may seem like chalk and cheese. What the comparison teaches, however, is that any organization that functions normally, day in day out, is an example of repeated success. The comparison also shows that inordinate risk-taking need not involve overt recklessness or volitional 'last chance saloon' style gambles. In the case of London Underground, inordinate risk-taking rested in the tacit assumption that fires below ground were inevitable and not particularly serious events (Fennell 1988). Barings was insufficiently rigorous in analysing what 'essentially' risk-free trading actually meant. By sparing itself from this task, it ended up stretching its definition of what constituted risk free. To paraphrase Starbuck and Millken (1988), the lesson for practice is that if organizations keep fine-tuning the odds, eventually something breaks, whether it's a disastrous options contract, a piece of rail track, an oil pipeline, or a contaminated bar of chocolate.

Would risk management have saved Barings?

Barings was criticized by the Board of Banking Supervision (1995) for not utilizing techniques of risk management. Since then risk management has virtually become an industry with managers spending hours of their time poring over charts and studying boxes variously shaded red, amber and green. We will never know whether it would have made any difference to Barings. I suspect not. In fact, as action generators, techniques of risk management might have made collapse *more* probable. Recall Starbuck's (1983) point that action generators are seldom updated with sufficient frequency. Risk registers focus attention upon risks that are officially acknowledged as posing a potential threat to the organization – to the exclusion of risks that exist but are out with the framework. Since such risks are not officially recognized, no one devotes any attention to them until a crisis erupts. Leeson's trading would hardly have occupied a prominent position on the risk register because it was deemed to be virtually risk free. In all likelihood the 'risk' would have been shaded green, that is, problem officially designated as under control because positions were matched. Just as once a blanket is thrown over a victim pronounced dead at the scene of a disaster no one is likely to lift the blanket to check whether the person might be alive, managers seldom spend long revisiting the issues shaded green. It is all they can do to deal with the 'ambers' and the 'reds'.

Members of ALCO might have argued among themselves about whether there was a funding risk and/or a reputational risk attached to Leeson's trading and if so whether those risks should be shaded red or amber on a sub-register. The argument might have been resolved by compromising on a dark shade of amber but what difference would it have made? Techniques of risk management have their place but they can lull managers into a false sense of security by making them think that they have covered all eventualities, conducted a rigorous analysis and asked the right questions.

In other words, such techniques impart an air of rationality to proceedings. Recall that while in theory rationality acts as a guide, it may be more accurate to see it as an achievement, as a symbolic product shot with non-rational influences (Brown 1989; see also Drummond 2001). The danger is that the language of management and in particular the images used (analysis, prioritization, balanced scorecard and so forth) can give a misleading impression of scientific objectivity calculated to conceal incertitude, political machinations, inflated egos and irresponsible mischief (further discussed in an IT context in Hirschheim and Newman 1991).

What is real?

Leeson (1996) says colleagues wanted to believe it was all true. Conventional theories of management depict organizations as scanning the environment looking for threats and opportunities. In this view, what organizations perceive to be 'reality' is virtually a mirror image of what is actually 'out there'. It may be more accurate, however, for managers to see organizations as creating their environments according to how information is received via action generators and then acting as if their creations were forcing them to act in a particular way – as ultimately they are (Weick 1979; see also Drummond 2001). Taking such a perspective makes it easier to distinguish between perception and reality or at least to remember that the two may not be synonymous.

A gap exists between myth and reality in all organizations. Many universities that define themselves as research led forget that their income comes mainly from teaching. Certain diseases like smallpox may be officially eradicated but that is not the same as saying that they are absolutely and utterly extinct. The lesson for management is to treat 'reality' as approximate, as 'useful fiction' when it comes to making decisions. The same goes for data. Effective management is not about having the most information or the most sophisticated analyses but being able to sense the *limits* of one's data, to see them not as literal reality but as 'liars in service of truth' (Brown 1977; Drummond 2001).

As early as 1985, long before the days of the internet and email, Karl Weick warned managers against the dangers of over-reliance upon machine-processed data and advised managers to seek out more intuitive information to augment the picture. It is good advice. When Peter Norris visited Singapore in mid-February, the computer printout of Leeson's reported revenues told one story. The sweating bilious person sitting opposite told another.

It is not what one's information reveals that matters so much as what it conceals. The management letter issued by the external auditors gave no hint of trouble in Singapore because the auditors were persuaded to omit mention of the SLK transaction. Such negotiations are by no means unusual. In some organizations employees plead with external auditors not to say anything that might reflect adversely upon them for fear of sanctions. Negotiations of a similar nature happen constantly in organizations. Health and Safety inspectors, for example, may be persuaded to 'go easy' on a particular hazard; project managers may be persuaded to 'stretch a point' and sign off work that is only partially complete. Managers should be alert to the possibility that things are not always what they seem to be. Moreover, when analysing their information, they should ask themselves what may have been left out.

If we have a vested interest in seeing a situation in a particular light, our judgement is likely to be biased. Reframing can help get issues into perspective. For example, when decisions are framed as a choice between losses, reframe the issue to identify best return on investment for the future. When past and present seem similar – look for differences. Recall the ill-fated brewery acquisition (Wilson et al. 1996). Both organizations produced beer but even the most superficial analysis would have shown that was where the comparison between the small plant and the big plant ended. Removing one's ego from the equation may prove more difficult. Boutique firms like Barings can survive against giant competitors but not by trying to emulate them. (See, for example, Starbuck's (1993) very interesting study of a small American law firm whose profits really did outstrip many of the giants.) Ego may have prevented Barings from reframing issues. For example, instead of asking how Leeson was making so much money and repeating familiar explanations, Barings might have posed a subtly different question, namely, 'Is it likely that Leeson is breaking the rules?'

Much was said after Barings collapsed about the dangers of trading exotic financial contracts (derivatives) (e.g. Stonham 1996a). The issue is a red herring in that it was mismanagement that brought Barings down rather than derivatives trading per se. Even so, this book shows what can happen when senior managers do not fully understand the business they are in (see also Board of Banking Supervision 1995). When we ask a question, we risk appearing momentarily foolish. When we refrain from asking, we risk incurring a much greater loss in the long run.

This book also shows how assumption can shade into fact. The first thing that the task force assembled by Peter Norris on 23 February 1995 did when they received the faxed copy of account 88888 was to try to match Osaka positions with positions on SIMEX:

> But it made no sense . . . Norris was now pacing the room, waiting for them to add up the futures. He looked over their shoulders to see what they were doing, and saw they were trying to match the positions. 'Bloody hell, you can't assume that. Just add it up!' he said.
>
> (Gapper and Denton 1995: 23)

Distinguished political scientists Neustadt and May (1986) suggest that managers can substantially reduce the risk of decision error by classifying information into 'known', 'unclear' and 'assumed'. It is good advice provided we remember that the most dangerous category of information is the 'known'. In organizations once something becomes accepted as fact, it becomes taken for granted. It is like throwing a blanket over a victim pronounced dead at the scene of an accident. With so many other cases to attend to, no one is likely to raise the blanket to check the person is actually dead. Everyone knew that Leeson's positions were matched. Once that assumption was dropped, everything became clear in an instant. If I could draw only one lesson from the Barings story it is this: it is not uncertainty that should worry us most but that of which we are rock solid certain.

References

Abolafia, M. Y. and Kilduff, M. (1988) 'Enacting market crisis: the social construction of a speculative bubble', *Administrative Science Quarterly*, 33, 177–93.

Allison, G. and Zelikow, P. (1999) *Essence of Decision: Explaining the Cuban Missile Crisis*, New York: Longman.

Arnold, P. J. and Sikka, P. (2001) 'Globalization and the state-profession relationship: the case the bank of Credit and Commerce International', *Accounting Organizations and Society*, 26, 475–99.

Auger, P. (2001) *The Death of Gentlemanly Capitalism*, Harmondsworth: Penguin.

Bachrach, P. and Baratz, M. S. (1963) 'Decisions and non-decisions: an analytical framework', *American Political Science Review*, 57, 632–42.

Banaji, M. R. and Greenwald, A. G. (1995) 'Implicit gender stereotyping in judgements of fame', *Journal of Personality and Social Psychology*, 68, 181–98.

Banaji, M. R., Bazerman, M. H. and Chugh, D. (2003) 'How (un)ethical are you?', *Harvard Business Review*, 81(12), 56–64.

Barley, S. R. (1983) 'Semiotics and the study of occupational and organizational cultures', *Administrative Science Quarterly*, 28, 393–413.

Barley, S. R. (1986) 'Technology as an occasion for structuring: evidence from observations of CT scanners and social order of radiology departments', *Administrative Science Quarterly*, 31, 78–108.

Barley, S. R. and Tolbert, P. S. (1997) 'Institutionalization and structuration: studying the links between action and institution', *Organization Studies*, 18, 93–118.

Barnard, C. (1938) *The Functions of the Executive*, Cambridge, MA: Harvard University Press.

Barrett, M. and Walsham, G. (1999) 'Electronic trading and work transformation in the London insurance market', *Information Systems Research*, 10, 1–22.

Bazerman, M. H. (2001) *Judgement in Managerial Decision-Making*, New York: Wiley.

Bazerman, M. H. (2005) 'Conducting influential research: the need for prescriptive implications', *Academy of Management Review*, 30(1), 25–31.

Bazerman, M. H., Beekun, R. I. and Schoorman, F. D. (1982) 'Performance evaluation in a dynamic context: a laboratory study of the impact of the prior commitment to the ratee', *Journal of Applied Psychology*, 67, 873–76.

Bazerman, M. H., Morgan, K. P. and Lowenstein, G. F. (1997) 'The impossibility of auditor independence', *Sloan Management Review*, 38(4), 89–94.

Bazerman, M. H., Moore, D. A., Tetlock, P. E. and Tanlu, L. (2006) 'Reports of solving the conflicts of interest in auditing are highly exaggerated', *Academy of Management Review*, 31(1), 43–49.

Becker, H. S. (1960) 'Notes on the concept of commitment', *American Journal of Sociology*, 66, 32–40.

Bingham, The Right Honourable Lord Justice (1992) *Inquiry into the Supervision of The Bank of Credit and Commerce International*, London: HMSO.

Blau, P. M. (1956) *Bureaucracy in Modern Society*, New York: Random.

Board of Banking Supervision (1995) *Report of the Inquiry into the Circumstances of the Collapse of Barings*, London: HMSO.

Bowen, M. G. (1987) 'The escalation phenomenon reconsidered: decision dilemmas or decision errors', *Academy of Management Review*, 12, 52–66.

Braverman, H. (1974) *Labour and Monopoly Capital*, New York: Monthly Review Press.

Brockner, J. (1992) 'The escalation of commitment to a failing course of action: toward theoretical progress', *Academy of Management Review*, 17, 39–61.

Brockner, J. and Houser, G. B. (1986) 'Escalation of commitment to an ineffective course of action: the effective of feedback having negative implications for self-identity', *Administrative Science Quarterly*, 31, 109–26.

Brockner, J., Rubin, J. Z. and Lang, E. (1981) 'Face-saving and entrapment', *Journal of Experimental Social Psychology*, 17, 68–79.

Brockner, J., Shaw, M. C. and Rubin J. Z. (1979) 'Factors affecting withdrawal from an escalating conflict: quitting before it's too late', *Journal of Experimental Social Psychology*, 17, 492–503.

Brown, A. D. (2005) 'Making sense of the collapse of Barings Bank', *Human Relations*, 58, 1579–604.

Brown, R. H. (1977) *A Poetic for Sociology*, Cambridge: Cambridge University Press.

Brown, R. H. (1978) 'Bureaucracy as praxis: toward a political phenomenology of formal organizations', *Administrative Science Quarterly*, 23, 365–82.

Brown, R. H. (1989) *Social Science as Civic Discourse*, Chicago, IL: University of Chicago Press.

Burrell, G. and Morgan, G. (1979) *Sociological Paradigms and Organizational Analysis*, Chicago, IL: University of Chicago Press.

Cameron, K. S. and Quinn, R. E. (1988) 'Organizational paradox and transformation', in R. E. Quinn and K. S. Cameron (eds) *Paradox and Transformation: Toward a Theory of Change in Organization and Management*, Cambridge, MA: Ballinger.

Caminiti, S. (1987) 'He put the kick back into Coke', *Fortune*, 26 October, 48.

Chiasson, M. and Saunders, C. (2005) 'Reconciling diverse approaches to opportunity research using the structuration theory', *Journal of Business Venturing*, 20, 747–67.

Chief Medical Officer (2006) *Good Doctors, Safer Patients: Report by the Chief Medical Officer*, London: Department of Health.

Clegg, S. R. (1989) 'Radical revisions: power discipline and organizations', *Organization Studies*, 10, 97–115.

Crozier, M. (1964) *The Bureaucratic Phenomenon*, London: Tavistock.

Dalton, M. (1959) *Men Who Manage*, New York: Wiley.

Dandridge, T. C., Mitroff, I. and Joyce, W. F. (1980) 'Organizational symbolism: a topic to expand organizational analysis', *Academy of Management Review*, 5, 77–82.

Deal, T. and Kennedy, A. (1988) *Corporate Culture: The Rites and Rituals of Corporate Life*, Harmondsworth: Penguin.

Deming, E. (1986) *Out of the Crisis*, Cambridge: Cambridge University Press.

Downs, A. (1967) *Inside Bureaucracy*, Boston, MA: Little, Brown.

Drummond, H. (1994) 'Escalation in organizational decision-making: a case of recruiting an incompetent employee', *Journal of Behavioral Decision Making*, 7, 43–55.

Drummond, H. (1996) *Escalation in Decision-Making: The Tragedy of Taurus*, Oxford, Oxford University Press.

Drummond, H. (1998a) 'Go and say "we're shutting": ju jitsu as a metaphor for analysing resistance', *Human Relations*, 51, 1–19.

Drummond, H. (1998b) 'Is escalation always irrational?', *Organization Studies*, 19, 911–29.

Drummond, H. (2001) *The Art of Decision Making: Mirrors of Imagination, Masks of Science*, Chichester: Wiley.

Drummond, H. (2004) 'See you next week? A study of entrapment in a small business', *International Small Business Journal*, 22, 487–502.

Drummond, H. and Chell, E. (2002) 'Life's chances and choices, a study of entrapment in career decisions with reference to Becker's side bets theory', *Personnel Review*, 30, 186–202.

Dunegan, K. J. (1993) 'Framing, cognitive models and image theory: toward an understanding of a glass half full', *Journal of Applied Psychology*, 78, 419–503.

Economist (1995a) 'The collapse of Barings: a fallen star', *The Economist*, 4 March, 19–21.

Economist (1995b) 'Baring not quite all', *The Economist*, 22 July, 66.

Economist (1995c) 'Who lost Barings?', *The Economist*, 22 July, 16.

Edelman, M. (1971) *Politics as Symbolic Action*, Chicago, IL: Markham.

Eichenwald, K. (2005) *Conspiracy of Fools*, New York: Broadway.

Etzioni, A. (1968) *The Active Society*, New York: Free Press.

Evans, H. (1983) *Good Times, Bad Times*, London: Weidenfeld & Nicolson.

Fay, S. (1982) *Beyond Greed*, New York: Viking.

Fay, S. (1996) *The Collapse of Barings*, London: Arrow.

Feldman, M. S. (2000) 'Organizational routines as a source of continuous change', *Organization Science*, 41, 611–29.

Fennell, D. (1988) *Investigation into the King's Cross Underground Fire*, Cm 499, Report for the Department of Transport, London: HMSO.

Festinger, L. (1957) *A Theory of Cognitive Dissonance*, Evanston, IL: Row, Peterson.

Financial Times (1991) *Behind Closed Doors – BCCI: The Biggest Bank Fraud in History*, London: Financial Times.

Forlani, D. and Mullins, J. W. (2000) 'Perceived risks and choices in entrepreneurs' new venture decisions', *Journal of Business Venturing*, 15, 305–22.

Fox, F. and Staw, B. M. (1979) 'The trapped administrator: the effects of job insecurity and policy resistance upon commitment to a course of action', *Administrative Science Quarterly*, 24, 449–71.

Gapper, J. (1997) 'Sharp rebuke and three year ban for Barings' risk chief', *Financial Times*, 12 March.

Gapper, J. and Denton, N. (1996) *All that Glitters: The Fall of Barings*, London: Hamish Hamilton.

Gapper, J. and Pirie, M. (2005) 'The human lesson of Nick Leeson's fraud', *Financial Times*, 17 February.

Ghoshal, S. and Moran, P. (1996) 'Bad for practice: a critique of the transaction cost theory', *Academy of Management Review*, 21(1), 13–47.

Gibbs, R. W. (1993) 'Process and products in making sense of tropes', in A. Ortony (ed.) *Metaphor and Thought*, Cambridge: Cambridge University Press.

Giddens, A. (1979) *Central Problems in Social Theory*, London: Macmillan.

Giddens, A. (1984) *The Constitution of Society*, Cambridge: Polity.

Giddens, A. (1995) *Politics, Sociology and Social Theory*, Cambridge: Polity.

Gladwell, M. (2000) *The Tipping Point*, London: Abacus.

Goffman, E. (1967) *Interaction Ritual: Essays on Face-to-Face Behaviour*, New York: Pantheon.

Greener, I. (2006) 'Nick Leeson and the collapse of Barings Bank: socio-technical networks and the "rogue-trader"', *Organization*, 13, 421–41.

Griffiths, M. D. (1990) 'The cognitive psychology of gambling', *Journal of Gambling Studies*, 6, 31–43.

Habermas, J. (1988) *On the Logic of the Social Sciences*, Cambridge, MA: MIT Press.

Habermas, J. (1992) *Postmetaphysical Thinking*, Cambridge: Polity.

Hall, M. J. B. (1995) *A Review of the Board of Banking Supervision's Inquiry into the Collapse of Barings*, Loughborough University Banking Centre Research Paper, 92/95, Loughborough, UK.

Hardin, G. (1968) 'The tragedy of the commons', *Science*, 162, 1243–48.

Hatch, M. (1999) 'Exploring the empty spaces of organization: how improvisational jazz helps re-describe organization studies', *Organization Studies*, 20, 75–101.

Hedberg, B. and Jonsson, S. (1977) 'Strategy formulation as a discontinuous process', *International Studies of Management and Organization*, 7, 88–109.

Herr, M. (1977) *Dispatches*, London: Picador.

Hirschheim, R. and Newman, M. (1991) 'Symbolism and information systems development: myth metaphor and magic', *Information Systems Research*, 2, 29–62.

Hobson, D. (1991) *The Pride of Lucifer*, London: Mandarin.

Hofstede, G. (1994) *Culture in Organizations*, London: HarperCollins.

Hoyos, C., Michaels, A. and Parker, A. (2004a) 'Regulators dig deeper into Royal Dutch/Shell's problems', *Financial Times*, 25 August, 21.

Hoyos, C., Michaels, A. and Parker, A. (2004b) 'Shell was warned on reserves in 2000', *Financial Times*, 25 August, 1.

Janis, I. L. (1982) *Groupthink*, London: Houghton Mifflin.

Janis, I. L. (1989) *Crucial Decisions: Leadership in Policy and Crisis Management*, New York: Free Press.

Janney, J. J. and Dess, G. G. (2004) 'Can real-options analysis improve decision-making? Promises and pitfalls', *Academy of Management Executive*, 18, 60–75.

Jelinek, M., Smircich, L. and Hirsch, P. (1983) 'Introduction: a code of many colours', *Administrative Science Quarterly*, 28, 331–38.

Kahneman, D. and Tversky, A. (1972) 'Subjective probability: a judgement of representativeness', *Cognitive Psychology*, 3, 430–54.

Kahneman, D. and Tversky, A. (1979) 'Prospect theory: an analysis of decision under risk', *Econometrica*, 47, 263–91.

Kahneman, D. and Tversky, A. (1982) 'The psychology of preferences', *Scientific American*, 246, 162–70.

Keiser, A. (1987) 'From asceticism to administration of wealth. Medieval monasteries and the pitfalls of rationalization', *Organization Studies*, 8, 103–23.

Kerr, N. L. and Tindale, R. S. (2003) 'Group performance and decision-making', *Annual review of Psychology*, 55, 623–55.

Knights, D. and Roberts, J. (1982) 'The power of organization or the organization of power?', *Organization Studies*, 3, 47–63.

Kramer, K. R. (1998) 'Re-visiting the Bay of Pigs and Vietnam decisions 25 years later: how well has the groupthink hypothesis stood the test of time?', *Organizational Behavior and Human Decision Processes*, 73, 236–71.

Kuhn, T. S. (1970) *The Structure of Scientific Revolutions*, Chicago, IL: University of Chicago Press.

Kynaston, D. (1994) *The City of London: A World of its Own, 1815–1890*, London: Chatto & Windus.

Kynaston, D. (2001) *The City of London: (Vol. IV) A Club No More, 1945–2000*, London: Chatto & Windus.

Lammers, C. J. (1988) 'The inter-organizational control of an occupied country', *Administrative Science Quarterly*, 33, 438–57.

Langer, E. J. (1983) *The Psychology of Control*, Beverly Hills, CA: Sage.

Lapierre, D. and Moro, J. (1997) *Five Past Midnight in Bhopal*, London: Simon and Schuster.

Larsen, P. T. (2005a) 'Barings – 10 years on', *Financial Times*, 19 February, 3.

Larsen, P. T. (2005b) 'Rogue traders still pose a threat', *Financial Times*, 21 February, 22.

Laudon, K. C. and Laudon, J. P. (1999) *Essentials of Management Information Systems*, Englewood Cliffs, NJ: Prentice Hall.

Leeson, N. with Whitley, E. (1997) *Rogue Trader*, London: Warner.

McCarthy, A. M., Schoorman, F. D. and Cooper, A. C. (1993) 'Reinvestment decisions by entrepreneurs – rational decision making or escalation of commitment', *Journal of Business Venturing*, 8, 9–24.

Mackintosh, J. (2001) 'City imposes life ban on Flaming Ferraris', *Financial Times*, 27 July.

McLean, B. and Elkind, P. (2003) *The Smartest Guys in the Room*, New York: Portfolio.

Manning, P. K. (1979) 'Metaphors of the field: varieties of organizational discourse', *Administrative Science Quarterly*, 24, 660–67.

March, J. G. (1981) 'Footnotes to organizational change', *Administrative Science Quarterly*, 26, 563–77.

Mars, G. (1982) *Cheats at Work: An Anthropology of Workplace Crime*, London: Allen & Unwin.

Mechanic, D. (1962) 'Sources of power of lower participants in complex organizations', *Administrative Science Quarterly*, 7, 349–64.

Meglino, B. M. and Korsgaard, M. A. (2004) 'Considering rational self-interest as a disposition: organizational implications of other orientation', *Journal of Applied Psychology*, 89, 946–59.

Merton, R. K. (1936) 'The unanticipated consequences of purposive social action', *American Sociological Review*, 1, 894–904.

Merton, R. K. (1948) 'The self-fulfilling prophecy', *Antioch Review*, 8, 193–210.

Merton, R. K. (1957) *Social Theory and Social Structure*, New York: Free Press.

Meyer, J. W. and Rowan, B. (1978) 'Institutionalized organizations: formal structure as myth and ceremony', *American Journal of Sociology*, 83, 340–63.

Miller, D. (1992) *The Icarus Paradox*, New York: Harper.

Ministry for Finance, Singapore (1995) *Barings Futures (Singapore) Pte Ltd: The Report of the Inspectors Appointed by the Minister for Finance*. Singapore: Ministry for Finance.

Mintzberg, H. (1993) 'Crafting strategy', in H. Mintzberg and J. B. Quinn (eds) *The Strategy Process*, Englewood Cliffs, NJ: Prentice Hall.

Moon, H. (2001) 'The two phases of conscientiousness: duty and achievement striving in escalation of commitment dilemmas', *Journal of Applied Psychology*, 86, 533–40.

Moon, H., Hollenbeck, J. R., Humphrey, S. E. and Maue, B. (2003) 'The tripartite model of neuroticism and the suppression of depression and anxiety within an escalation of commitment dilemma', *Journal of Personality*, 71, 347–67.

Moore, D. A., Tetlock, P. E., Tanlu, L. and Bazerman, M. H. (2006) 'Conflicts of interest and the case of auditor independence: moral seduction and strategic issue cycling', *Academy of Management Review*, 31(1), 10–29.

Morgan, G. (1980) 'Paradigms, metaphors and puzzle solving in organizations', *Administrative Science Quarterly*, 25, 605–22.

Morgan, G. (1983) 'More on metaphor: why we cannot control tropes in administrative science', *Administrative Science Quarterly*, 28: 601–07.

Morgan, G. (1990) 'Paradigm diversity in organizational research', in J. Hassard and D. Pym (eds) *The Theory and Philosophy of Organizations*, London: Routledge.

Morgan, G. (1996) *Images of Organization*, London: Sage.

Morgan, G., Frost, P. J. and Pondy, L. R. (1983) 'Organizational symbolism', in L. R. Pondy, P. J. Frost, G. Morgan and T. C. Dandridge (eds) *Organizational Symbolism*, London: JAI Press.

National Commission on Terrorist Attacks (2004) *The 9/11 Commission Report: Final Report of the National Commission on Terrorist Attacks upon the United States*, New York: Norton.

Neustadt, R. E. and May, E. R. (1986) *Thinking in Time: The Uses of History for Decision-Makers*, New York: Free Press.

O'Neill, S. and McGrory, D. (2006) *The Suicide Factory: Abu Hamza and the Finsbury Park Mosque*, London: Harper.

Orlikowski, W. J. (1996) 'Improvising organizational transformation over time: a situated change perspective', *Information Systems Research*, 7, 63–92.

Ouchi, W. G. (1980) 'Markets, bureaucracies and clans', *Administrative Science Quarterly*, 25, 129–41.

Pascale, R. T. and Athos, A. G. (1982) *The Art of Japanese Management*, Harmondsworth: Penguin.

Perrow, C. (1984) *Normal Accidents: Living with High Risk Technologies*, New York: Basic Books.

Peters, T. J. (1978) 'Symbols, patterns and settings: an optimistic case for getting things done', *Organizational Dynamics*, 7, 2–23.

Peters, T. J. and Waterman, R. H. (1982) *In Search of Excellence: Lessons from America's Best-Run Companies*, New York: Harper & Row.

Pettigrew, A. M. (1972) *The Politics of Organizational Decision-Making*, London: Tavistock.

Pettigrew, A. M. (1979) 'On studying organizational cultures', *Administrative Science Quarterly*, 24, 570–640.

Pfeffer, J. (1977) 'The ambiguity of leadership', *Academy of Management Review*, 2, 104–12.

Pfeffer, J. (1981) 'Management as symbolic action: the creation and maintenance of organizational paradigms', in L. L. Cumings and B. M. Staw (eds) *Research in Organizational Behavior*, Greenwich, CT: JAI Press.

Pfeffer, J. (1992) *Managing with Power: Politics and Influence in Organizations*, Boston, MA: Harvard Business School Press.

Pfeffer, J. and Fong, C. T. (2005) 'Building organization theory from first principles: the self-enhancement motive and understanding power and influence', *Organization Science*, 16, 372–88.

Pharo, C. (1995) 'Leeson's boss at Barings quizzed', *The Sun*, 1 March, 1 and 7.

Platt, J. (1973) 'Social traps', *American Psychologist*, 28, 641–51.

Power, M. (1997) *The Audit Society*, Oxford: Oxford University Press.

Rawnsley, J. (1996) *Going for Broke: Nick Leeson and the Collapse of Barings Bank*, London: HarperCollins.

Ray, C. A. (1986) 'Corporate culture: the last frontier of control', *Journal of Management Studies*, 23, 287–99.

Reich, C. (1980) 'The confessions of Siegmund Warburg', *Institutional Investor*, March, 167–201.

Riley, P. (1983) A structurationist account of political culture', *Administrative Science Quarterly*, 28, 414–37.

Ritzer, G. (1993) *The McDonaldization of Society*, London: Pine Forge Press.

Ross, J. (1997) 'Rogue Trader: How I Brought Down Barings Bank and Shook the Financial World, by Nick Leeson, Boston: Little Brown, 1996', *Academy of Management Review*, 22, 1006–10.

Ross, J. and Staw, B. M. (1986) 'Expo 86: an escalation prototype', *Administrative Science Quarterly*, 31, 379–91.

Ross, J. and Staw, B. M. (1993) 'Organizational escalation and exit: lessons from the Shoreham nuclear power plant', *Academy of Management Journal*, 36, 701–32.

Rubin, J. Z. and Brockner, J. (1975) 'Factors affecting entrapment in waiting situations: the Rosencrantz and Guildenstern effect', *Journal of Personality and Social Psychology*, 31, 1054–63.

Rudolph, J. W. and Repenning, N. R. (2002) 'Disaster dynamics: understanding the role of quantity in organizational collapse', *Administrative Science Quarterly*, 47, 1–29.

Salancik, G. R. (1977) 'Commitment is too easy', *Organizational Dynamics*, 6, 62–80.

Salancik, G. R. and Pfeffer, J. (1977) 'Who gets power – and how they hold on to it: a strategic contingency model of power', *Organizational Dynamics*, 5, 2–21.

Sarason, V., Dean, T. and Dillard, J. F. (2006) 'Entrepreneurship as the nexus of individual and opportunity', *Journal of Business Venturing*, 21, 286–305.

Schaubroeck, J. and Williams, S. (1993) 'Type A behaviour pattern and escalating commitment', *Journal of Applied Psychology*, 5, 862–67.

Schoorman, F. D. (1988) 'Escalation bias in performance appraisals: an unintended consequence of supervisor participation in hiring decisions', *Journal of Applied Psychology*, 73, 58–62.

'Secretary of State's case against Mr Baker', *In the High Court of Justice Chancery Division*, 3 March 1998.

'Secretary of State's case against Mr Gamby', *In the High Court of Justice Chancery Division*, 3 March 1998.

'Secretary of State's case against Mr Tuckey', *In the High Court of Justice Chancery Division*, 3 March 1998.

Shaw, M. E. (1981) *Group Dynamics*, New York: McGraw-Hill.

Simons, D. J. and Chabris, C. F. (1999) 'Gorillas in our midst: sustained inattentional blindness for dynamic events', *Perception*, 28, 1059–74.

Sitkin, S. B. and Pablo, A. L. (1992) 'Re-conceptualizing the determinants of risk behaviour', *Academy of Management Review*, 17, 9–39.

Sitkin, S. B. and Weingart, L. R. (1995) 'Determinants of risky decision-making behaviour: a test of the mediating role of risk perceptions and propensity', *Academy of Management Journal*, 38, 1573–93.

Smircich, L. (1983) 'Concepts of culture and organizational analysis', *Administrative Science Quarterly*, 28, 339–58.

Smith, A. (1983) *The Wealth of Nations*, Harmondsworth: Penguin.

Starbuck, W. H. (1983) 'Organizations as action generators', *American Sociological Review*, 48, 91–102.

Starbuck, W. H. (1993) 'Keeping a butterfly and elephant in a house of cards: the elements of exceptional success', *Journal of Management Studies*, 30, 885–921.

Starbuck, W. H. and Millken, F. J. (1988) 'Challenger: fine-tuning the odds until something breaks', *Journal of Management Studies*, 25, 319–40.

Staw, B. M. (1976) 'Knee-deep in the big muddy: a study of escalating commitment to a chosen course of action', *Organizational Behaviour and Human Performance*, 16, 27–44.

Staw, B. M. (1981) 'The escalation of commitment to a course of action', *Academy of Management Review*, 6, 577–87.

Staw, B. M. (1997) 'Escalation research: an update and appraisal', in Z. Shapira (ed.) *Organizational Decision Making*, Cambridge: Cambridge University Press.

Staw, B. M. and Hoang, H. (1995) 'Sunk costs in the NBA: why draft order affects playing time', *Administrative Science Quarterly*, 40, 474–94.

Staw, B. M. and Ross, J. (1987) 'Behaviour in escalation situations: antecedents, prototypes and solutions', in L. L. Cummings and B. M. Staw (eds) *Research in Organization Behaviour*, London: JAI Press.

Staw, B. M., Sandelands, L. E. and Dutton, J. E. (1981) 'Threat rigidity effects in organizational behavior: a multi-level analysis', *Administrative Science Quarterly*, 26, 501–24.

Stein, M. (2000) 'The risk-taker as shadow: a psychoanalytic view of the collapse of Barings', *Journal of Management Studies*, 37, 1215–59.

Sterba, R. L. A. (1978) 'Clandestine management in the imperial Chinese bureaucracy', *Academy of Management Review*, 3, 67–78.

Stern, C. (1997) *Dr Iain West's Casebook*, London: Warner.

Stonham, P. (1996a) 'Whatever happened at Barings? Part One: The lure of derivatives and collapse', *European Management Journal*, 14(2), 167–75.

Stonham, P. (1996b) 'Whatever happened at Barings? Part Two: Unauthorised trading and the failure of controls', *European Management Journal*, 14(2), 269–78.

Stoppard, T. (1967) *Rosencrantz and Guildenstern are Dead*, London: Faber & Faber.

Tait, N. (2005) 'Bank refused to settle BCCI case', *Financial Times*, 5 October.

Taylor, F. W. (1947) *Scientific Management*, New York: Harper & Row.

Taylor, S. E. (1980) *Positive Illusions*, New York: Basic Books.

Teger, A. I. (1980) *Too Much Invested to Quit: The Psychology of the Escalation of Conflict*, New York: Pergamon.

Treasury Committee (1996a) *Barings Bank and International Regulation: Minutes of Evidence*, 15 May, London: HMSO.

Treasury Committee (1996b) *Barings Bank and International Regulation: Minutes of Evidence*, 10 June 1996, London: HMSO.

Treasury Committee (1996c) *Barings Bank and International Regulation: Minutes of Evidence*, 23 July, London: HMSO.

Treasury Committee (1996d) *Barings Bank and International Regulation: Minutes of Evidence*, Mr Hopkins and Mr Baker, 23 July, London: HMSO.

Uzzi, B. (1997) 'Social structure and competition in inter-firm networks: the paradox of embeddedness', *Administrative Science Quarterly*, 42, 35–67.

Uzzi, B. (1999) 'Embeddedness in the making of financial capital', *American Sociological Review*, 64, 481–505.

Watson, T. (1994) *In Search of Management: Culture Chaos and Control in Managerial Work*, London: Routledge.

Watzlawick, P. (1976) *How Real is Real?* New York: Norton.

Watzlawick, P. (1988) *Ultra-solutions, or, How to Fail Most Successfully*, New York: Norton.

Watzlawick, P. (1993) *The Situation is Hopeless but not Serious*, New York: Norton.

Watzlawick, P., Weakland, J. H. and Fisch, R. (1974) *Change: Principles of Problem Formation and Resolution*, New York: Norton.

Weber, M. (1947) *The Theory of Economic and Social Organization*, Oxford: Oxford University Press.

Wechsberg, J. (1967) *The Merchant Bankers*, London: Weidenfeld & Nicolson.

Weick, K. E. (1979) *The Social Psychology of Organizing*, Reading, MA: Addison-Wesley.

Weick, K. E. (1985) 'Cosmos vs chaos: sense and nonsense in electronic contexts', *Organizational Dynamics*, 14, 50–64.

Weick, K. E. (1988) 'Enacted sense making in organizations', *Journal of Management Studies*, 25, 305–17.

Weick, K. E. (1990) 'The vulnerable system: an analysis of the Tenerife air disaster', *Journal of Management*, 6, 571–93.

Weick, K. E. (1993) 'The collapse of sense-making in organizations: the Mann Gulch disaster', *Administrative Science Quarterly*, 38, 628–52.

Weick, K. E. (1995) *Sense Making in Organizations*, Beverly Hills, CA: Sage.

Whyte, G. (1986) 'Escalating commitment to a course of action: a re-interpretation', *Academy of Management Review*, 11, 311–21.

Whyte, G. (1991a) 'Diffusion of responsibility: effects on the escalation tendency', *Journal of Applied Psychology*, 76, 408–15.

Whyte, G. (1991b) 'Decision failures: why they occur and how to prevent them', *Academy of Management Executive*, 5, 23–32.

Whyte, G., Saks, A. M. and Hook, S. (1997) 'When success breeds failure: the art of self-efficacy in escalating commitment to a losing course of action', *Journal of Organizational Behaviour*, 18, 415–32.

Wilkins, A. L. and Ouchi, W. G. (1983) 'Efficient cultures: exploring the relationship between culture and organizational performance', *Administrative Science Quarterly*, 28, 468–81.

Williamson, O. E. (1975) *Markets and Hierarchies: Analysis and Anti-trust Implications*, New York: Free Press.

Williamson, O. E. (1981) 'The economics of organization: the transaction cost approach', *American Journal of Sociology*, 87, 548–77.

Williamson, O. E. (1991) 'Comparative economic organization: the analysis of discrete structural alternatives', *Administrative Science Quarterly*, 36, 269–96.

Willmott, H. (1993) 'Strength is ignorance; slavery is freedom: managing culture in modern organization', *Journal of Management Studies*, 30, 515–52.

Wilson, D. C., Hickson, D. J. and Miller, S. (1996) 'How organizations can over-balance: decision overreach as a reason for failure', *American Behavioral Scientist*, 39, 995–1010.

Wing, R. L. (1988) *The Tao of Power*, London: Thorsons.

Wong, K. F. E. (2005) 'The role of risk in making decisions under escalation situations', *Applied Psychology: An International Review*, 54, 584–607.

Wrong, D. H. (1979) *Power: Its Forms, Bases and Uses*, Oxford: Basil Blackwell.

Yates, J. F. and Stone, E. R. (1992) 'Risk appraisal', in J. F. Yates (ed.) *Risk-Taking Behavior*, New York: Wiley.

Zander, M. (1982) *Making Groups Effective*, San Francisco, CA: Jossey Bass.

Zardkoohi, A. (2004) 'Do real options lead to escalation of commitment?', *Academy of Management Review*, 29, 111–19.

Ziegler, P (1988) *The Sixth Great Power: Barings 1762–1929*, London: Collins.

Index